A BASKET FULL OF
Miracles

PAULETTE E. CARELLI

A BASKET FULL OF MIRACLES

ISBN-13: 978-1-77069-134-6

Printed in Canada.

Word Alive Press
131 Cordite Road, Winnipeg, MB R3W 1S1
www.wordalivepress.ca

Library and Archives Canada Cataloguing in Publication

Carelli, Paulette E., 1949-
        A basket full of miracles / Paulette E. Carelli.

ISBN 978-1-77069-134-6

        1. Carelli, Paulette E., 1949-. 2. Carelli, Domenic, 1933-.
3. Christian biography--Canada. I. Title.

BR1725.C37A3 2010   248.4   C2010-907226-X

Manon

*Thank you for taking such care
for my darling
Paulette.*

dedications

I would like to dedicate this book to the people who have walked through its pages.

Linda Hamilton, for all your prayers and help.

Stephen Lund, for helping type my final draft.

To my two sons, who are my heart—Steven Dunn and Paul Dunn.

To my four stepchildren—Frank, Marisa, Domenica, and Tony, who have made their way into my heart.

And to my grandchildren—Whitley Dunn, Jack and Sadie Carelli, Melina Moro, and Domenic and Amanda Fabrig. This is your legacy.

To my sister, Gaile Larosie—our search for each other has ended. We now understand God's unconditional love.

And to my niece, Debby Armstrong, who has always been one of my children.

I thank you, Heavenly Father, for sending us your son, to make all things possible in *His Name*.

All have added to who I am
today and all will be in my
prayers with the hope for
our tomorrows.

Reach into the basket of life
and find hope, forgiveness, and
peace through our Lord and
Saviour.

Jesus will lift up the basket
to be filled and to be blessed
by God.

contents

BOOK ONE

BOOK TWO

BOOK
1

*"We, too, must feed the hungry
by sharing Jesus with the world."*
—PAULETTE CARELLI

introduction

From Matthew 14:13–21

As evening approached, the disciples of Jesus came to him and said, "This is a remote place. Send the crowds away to the village to buy food."

Jesus replied, "Give them something to eat."

"We have only five loaves of bread and two fish," they answered.

"Bring them to me," he said.

Jesus looked up into heaven and gave thanks to his father for the food before him. Jesus then broke this offering into smaller pieces. The disciples passed out enough food to feed five thousand people. The disciples did not understand or have faith that Jesus was able to supply the needs of the crowd.

This was a miracle of God. We can ask ourselves what miracles are. I believe they happen every day. We are eager to explain them away. People use this term loosely or apply humour while seeing or experiencing things beyond their comprehension.

I've come to know that a miracle is a happening that reaches into the realms of life beyond our understanding, ability, or control. What makes a person's life experience worth putting down on paper? I hear people talking about themselves and I readily ask, what makes them unique? What is unique is how people handle these experiences. Finding the driving force within themselves makes the difference. This will tug on my heart, bring me to my knees, and certainly draw my interest.

Like the disciples distributing the loaves and fishes, I have been led and encouraged to distribute my story to those who will listen. As I raise my basket full of miracles to heaven, I am reminded of the faithfulness of our heavenly Father to bless his children. Hungry, anyone?

one

DAY OF RECKONING

June 6, 1976

*t*he doorbell rang and before me stood a well-dressed and striking gentleman. He introduced himself as a pastor from an intercity church. He was recruiting children to attend Sunday school.

I was painting my living room and, by the looks of me, my clothes as well. I threw on a housecoat before opening the door. I told this man I had the flu and hoped he would go away.

He invited himself in and we began to talk, or should I say *he* talked—and talked. I offered him a coffee, tea, or beer. Ding, ding. Two strikes against me. What I didn't know was that he was all prayed up. His visit was blessed by God. I didn't have a chance. He was on a mission and he delivered the goods.

He asked me questions about my family and myself in order to establish common ground. How could I tell this stranger that I was remarried and seeking deliverance from the occult? I knew nothing about the weapons of spiritual warfare or the power of the blood of Jesus Christ. There was a stronghold against my family, my home, and myself.

I sought help, but nobody knew how to help.

♦   ♦   ♦

I need to take you back several years. You will soon understand why I named this book *A Basket Full of Miracles*.

I was raised in a home where alcohol took its toll. My sister and I witnessed different levels of abuse. My sister was bold, meeting difficulties straight on. I myself would curl up in a corner and pray it would all go away. As a result, my sister was labelled rebellious and I was known as mommy's little pet. We both spent our lives looking for unconditional love, and it came with a price.

STUMBLING BLOCK

While watching a show called *Bewitched*, I became fascinated by its message. I would fantasize about changing my world with a twitch of my nose. If only life could be that easy. I had no idea that this make-believe world held a key into the occult.

MY SHIELD

My love for the Lord was a shield about me. When I was in Grade Two, I was taught by nuns. At one point, my whole class went to church to learn how to pray the Stations of the Cross. I was on my knees in prayer, reflecting on what Jesus had done for me on the cross, when I felt someone tap me on the shoulder, drawing me back to my surroundings.

"We do not play in church," my teacher said, talking down to me in a scolding tone. "You were told to line up with the other children when you were finished."

I was too intimidated to tell her I had only finished the third Station of the Cross. This incident left a mark on my spirit, yielding me to submit to control.

> The disciples came to Jesus and asked, "Who is the greatest in the kingdom of heaven?"
>
> He called a little child to him and had him stand among them. And he said, "I tell you the truth, unless you change and become like little children, you will never enter the kingdom of heaven. Therefore, whoever humbles himself like this child is the greatest in the kingdom of heaven. And whoever welcomes a little child like this in my name welcomes me. But if anyone causes one of these little ones who believe in me to sin, it would be better for him to have a large millstone hung

round his neck to be drowned in the
depths of the sea." (Matthew 18:1–5)

The moulding of a child's spirit will carry them
throughout their lifetime. Breaking a child's will can
destroy them.

Halloween

Many small children accompanied by their parents
came to our door asking for candy one particular Hal-
loween when I was a child, but some were collecting
money for UNICEF. These children had a small box in
their hands. There was a small hole in the top of the box
for people to drop money inside. The children asking
for money had a string around their neck with a tag
that said UNICEF, and their first name was also written
on the tag.

When the children left, I was so excited that I
wanted to help. But I didn't know how. I began looking
around the house for a small box. When I found one, I
began to prepare it with pictures of children I had cut
out of our magazines. I used my scissors to penetrate
the box, making a large hole on top. That way, people
would be able to give more money for the children.
Now I needed a tag to wear around my neck. I found
some wool in my mom's sewing box and cardboard
from a pair of my mom's nylons. I made my badge and
proudly placed it around my neck.

Off I went on a mission. I didn't carry a bag for
candy because I was focused on helping children I

knew nothing about. Going to my first door was frightening, but I was so excited. I stood straight and proud and held my box high so that people could see the children's faces.

The lady greeted me kindly and dropped a few coins into the box. I was so happy. I kept telling Jesus that I was helping him feed the children.

When I finished collecting money in my area, I ventured onto a block of homes unknown to me. A lady with a puzzled look on her face opened the door. She peered down at me and asked sharply, "What do you think you are doing?"

Then she called me a little thief. Me, a thief? Never, never! She said she was going to phone the neighbours and warn them about me. Then she said she was going to call the police and that I should be ashamed of myself.

I ran down her walkway and straight to my church. I spent a lot of time in that church, because I felt Jesus there. I knew this was Jesus' house and that he would take care of me.

To wilfully break the spirit of a child is wrong. I knelt down and cried. I couldn't understand what I had done to make this lady say those things. I tried to sort out her cruel words. I knew my motives were only to help others, and to call me a thief... she couldn't have been more wrong.

I looked for my priest, but he was nowhere in sight. I wanted to dispense of this money, so I looked around the church for an offering basket. I remembered putting offering money into an opening in the wall beside our Blessed Virgin's statue. I quickly dropped all the coins I collected through the hole, then left the collection box beside the statue. I lit the candle as I always had before when I came with my parents. Kneeling down, I asked Mary to make sure the money made its way to the children. Drying my tears, I made my way back home and never spoke of it again—until now.

> Blessed is the man who does not walk in the counsel of the wicked or stand in the way of sinners or sit in the seat of mockers. But his delight is in the law of the Lord, and on his law he meditates day and night. He is like a tree planted by streams of water, which yields its fruits in season and whose leaf does not wither. (Psalms 1:1–3)

If I knew the ways of God and chose to follow them, I knew life would be different. Parents need to counsel their children. Parents, pray before you respond to your children, seeking God's direction for their lives.

LACK OF KNOWLEDGE AND JUDGMENT

At the age of eighteen, I was married to a Canadian soldier who was ten years my senior. I didn't have the wisdom to know what makes a man tick. I never found out his past, never explored his temperament, and I certainly never knew I was to pray and ask God if this was the man for me before I married him. He carried extensive baggage from his childhood and together, without outside intervention, we were doomed to fail.

He never enjoyed talking or sharing. Even holding my hand was too much to hope for. I was starving for personal contact. After we were married, his older sister told me that he had ended a boy's life by hitting him over the head with a piece of wood during a fight. They were classmates in third grade. He had exhibited violence intermittently throughout his youth and beyond. This baggage was apparent in the hardships that existed in our marriage.

My first son was born nine months and fifteen days after we were wed. This precious baby gave me someone to hold, talk to, and laugh with. He became the focal point in my life. I poured all my love and energy into his life.

After two years of marriage, we were transferred to Germany. My husband went on before my son and me and we followed three months later. We traveled on a military plane, which should have been retired years earlier. It was so loud; it shook, clanged, and banged. It was hard to hear even the conversation going on next to me. I heard later that this plane was docked at a military base in Germany. Upon arrival, my husband—who had become a stranger to me—greeted my son and me. We completed our journey on a military bus. Two hours passed and few words were exchanged between us.

The Beginning of Our End

I would like to paint a visual picture so you can understand how loneliness can be a significant factor in changing a person's life.

As we approached the wartorn building in the centre of town, I felt panic. I quickly learned that we were going to live above a butcher shop where meat of all kinds was prepared and sold. The stench was noticeable upon entering the building. As we approached the front entrance, I was surprised to see it was protected by a cast-iron gate. This had been needed during the war years to protect the property and home. A large iron key was placed into the lock and the sound of screeching metal could be heard as the gate opened.

As we stepped onto the landing, a wooden door was unlocked, leading us into the landlady's apartment/shop. A set of stairs was directly in front of us, leading to one of the upper floors.

The community toilet, used by four families, was at the entry of our apartment. The washroom consisted of a miniature toilet and a window that overlooked the butcher's courtyard. If someone was tall, his or her knees would touch the door. Backing in was the only way to make use of this facility and washing your hands was not an option. Yuck!

Now I was able to go to our suite. Oh, wait! There was another door to unlock, and a ramp to cross with a direct drop below. At least the ramp had a railing to block the fall.

It was now time for our grand entrance. In front of me was the kitchen; my outstretched arms could reach both sides. There was no stove to clean, no fridge to defrost, but I did have a basket to lower out the window on a rope. This was to help keep our food fresh. I could only hope that a breeze would pass by and that an odour didn't accompany that breeze. I quickly learned portion control so that I didn't have leftovers at mealtime. I shopped daily, which was no problem because I lived downtown.

My kitchen sink was the size of a bathroom sink in Canada. We were allowed to bathe in our landlady's suite once a week. If more hygiene was required, well, I did the dishes first. Did I mention that we had no hot running water? My electric teakettle and two-burner hot plate gave me an ample supply of hot water. Diapers, dishes, clothes, and a small child—I was busy-busy!

Our living room had what seemed to be children's furniture in it; at least my legs touched my chest while sitting. I'm 5'2, so life was good. The view from our living room could have used a mural of a sun and blue sky; the apartment just a few feet away blocked out light.

Everyone has a favourite room in their house and mine was our eating area/bedroom. It was great. If a turkey dinner was eaten, we could dine and take a nap at the same time. Did I mention that the Army rejected this apartment, but my husband told them it would do for his family?

On a more serious note, this apartment became my prison. When our landlady was away and my husband was on military manoeuvres, I was frightened and very much alone... except for my son.

THE ARMOUR OF GOD

> Be strong in the Lord and in his mighty power. Put on the full armor of God so you that can take your stand against the devil's schemes. For our struggle is not against flesh and blood, but against the rulers, against the authorities, against the powers of the dark world and against the spiritual forces of evil in the heavenly realms. Therefore put on the full armor of God, so that when the day of evil comes, you may be able to stand your ground, and after you have done everything, to stand. Stand firm then, with the belt of truth buckled around your waist, with the breastplate of righteousness in place, and with your feet fitted with the readiness that comes from the gospel of peace. In addition to all this, take up a shield of faith, with which you can extinguish all the flaming arrows of the evil one. Take the helmet of salvation and the sword of the Spirit, which is the word of God. (Ephesians 6:10–17)

A soldier who goes on the battlefield unprepared, without his weapon cleaned and loaded, will likely be killed, as will those whose protection he is entrusted with. A soldier must know who his enemy is, unlike our human commanders who send our military into battle hoping they're doing the right thing. God knows all things. He is ready, able, and in control. Let Jesus go before you in all things. Give Christ ownership of your life and he promises to direct, protect, and bless your path.

Into Darkness

The nightmare began when we met people who found it entertaining to play around with the Ouija board. This is not a game. Spirits are being called upon to tell you things. In disobedience to God, the enemy took a stronghold on my life.

> Therefore, brothers, we have an obligation—but it is not to the sinful nature, to live according to it. For if you live according to the sinful nature, you'll die; but if by the Spirit you put to death the misdeeds of the body, you will live, because those who are led by the Spirit of God are sons of God. For you did not receive a spirit that makes you a slave again to fear, but you receive the Spirit of sonship. And by him we cry, "Abba, Father." The Spirit himself testifies with our spirit that we are God's children. Now if we are children, then we are heirs—heirs of God and co-heirs with Christ, if indeed we share in

> his sufferings in order that we may
> share in his glory. (Romans 8:12–17)
>
> Now to him who is able to do immeas-
> urably more than all we ask or imagine,
> according to his power that is at work
> within us. (Ephesians 3:20)

We can choose to reject God, as I did, and open the
way to the enemy to take a foothold. The Bible says he
is like a lion roaming the earth to see who he can devour.

BEFORE MY NEW LIFE IN CHRIST

I was watching a Christian talk show one day and was
ready to change the channel when I heard a rock singer
say, "The name Satan is a metaphor for the ultimate
form of rebellion." We know that Satan is not a metaphor; he is a real spirit who once served God, until he
wanted to be God himself. He was cast out of heaven
because of this total rebellion against God.

The demonic is real, and Satan has one way to hurt
God—by destroying our lives. When I was involved in
the occult, I felt like I was in a void. I can't put my experience into words. I was out of control... it's hard to
describe.

While I was in Germany, I befriended a spirit who
made himself known through the use of the Ouija
board. This spirit was from a man who had been mur-
dered in the apartment many years before. The land-

lady confirmed that there had been a murder in my apartment during the war years. Just think how desperate for a friend I was to befriend a spirit! Getting involved with spirits is never of God.

My son, Paul, suffered from my involvement with the occult. One day, when I was shopping, I felt an urgency to return home. Fear had come over me. I ran home and asked my landlady if Paul was okay. Things appeared to be all right. I quickly went over to where Paul was having his nap and, again, things appeared fine. I went to the living room to rest when I heard a man's voice saying, "Paulette, come here." Running to where Paul was sleeping, I heard the voice again. I saw that my little boy had a man's voice coming out of him. I was terrified. I knelt down, crying to God for help.

"Please God," I cried. "Don't let Paul suffer for what I've done."

Believe me. It is not a quick fix just to say, "Oops! Sorry, God."

JESUS AND BEELZEBUB

> Then they brought him a demon-possessed man who was blind and mute, and Jesus healed him... But when the Pharisees heard this, they said, "It is only by Beelzebub, the prince of demons, that this fellow drives out demons."
>
> Jesus knew their thoughts and said to them, "Every kingdom divided against itself will be ruined, and every

city or household divided against itself will not stand. If Satan drives out Satan, he is divided against himself. How then can his kingdom stand? And if I drive out demons by Beelzebub, by whom do your people drive them out? So then, they will be your judges. But if I drive out demons by the Spirit of God, then the kingdom of God has come upon you. Or again, how can anyone enter a strong man's house and carry off his possessions unless he first ties up the strong man?" (Matthew 12:22, 24–29)

TURNING POINT

My husband was mentally cruel and physically violent. I became pregnant and miscarried two months later. I asked my husband for help when I started to lose the baby. He refused to take me to the hospital. I had to go and get a babysitter for Paul, and my landlady took me to the hospital.

Upon my return home, I was bitter. I asked for a divorce and felt justified when I saw him crying over telling him our marriage had ended. For the first time in my life, I hated someone. It reminded me of how Pharaoh's heart was hardened against the Israelites. I had always had a tender heart. If someone cried a tear, I would cry, too. Now I was hardened of heart. I believed that it was the only thing that would get me through the months that followed.

We all returned to Canada. Paul and I stayed with my parents for two weeks until I was able to find an apartment. My mom's first response after my return was one of authority. She extended her arm and hand toward me saying, "I don't want to hear it." She never allowed me to express my heartbreak or my fears. Her wall was high and I never had the skills or strength to bring them down. I was tired of being on the battlefield.

My divorce was finalized fifteen months later.

EXCESS BAGGAGE

I moved on to my second husband while I was waiting for my divorce. I was damaged and confused, and I carried enough insecurity into my new marriage to sabotage any hopes we could have had.

Jim was, and still is, a gentle and quiet man. I needed someone to put me in my place with wisdom and the love I so desperately needed. One of the first things I said to Jim was, "You are not going to do to me what I let my last husband do." This man should have looked for the nearest door. We had many good years of marriage, but we grew apart. I poured myself into my ministries while he stayed at home and looked after our two sons.

I'm not going to write about what went wrong in our marriage. It wouldn't serve any purpose. We were divorced after twenty-four years of marriage and we left a lot of brokenness in our paths. We have since become casual friends and wish the best for each other.

Jim passed away in September 2009. Steven, our youngest son, was by his side. The love between these two men was humbling and inspiring. They were not only father and son, but also best friends.

In the latter two years of Jim's life, Steven took care of his dad. During the last three months, he even took Jim into his home and cared for his every need.

Jim often said, "Son, I'm sorry I'm such a burden."

This drove Steven crazy. Steven's response was, "Dad, it's my privilege and honour to care for you. Dad, you are my hero. I only hope I can be half the man you are."

Steven, your dad would be so proud of you. I know I am.

two

LOSING MY PEACE

i didn't know who I was anymore. My whole identity was wrapped up in my service to God and family. My loneliness and separation from God cast a dark shadow over my existence. I was also wishing to come to the cross. I knew Jesus was willing to forgive all who came to him, but first we must repent and turn from our ways. I just kept going forward, searching for peace. I wasn't satisfied with having only God's love. I desperately needed approval from mankind. Even in this search, I knew the only true peace would come from God.

I knew my heavenly Father in a personal way. He was and is as real to me as if I were talking to a person standing in front of me.

The ministry I had was anointed and blessed. I knew the leading of the Holy Spirit and understood the power of prayer. I put on the armour of God daily and tried to die to the flesh. Then I threw it all away. Yes, I am human, but—well, I can't put it into words or explain the loss I felt. My spiritual separation was more devastating than the separation of the human element.

> So, because you are lukewarm—neither hot nor cold—I am about to spit you out of my mouth. (Revelation 3:16)

This is why I found it difficult to praise God in front of other people. I felt like a hypocrite. I couldn't lift my arms in praise or worship. I couldn't be a hypocrite. I loved my Lord too much to disgrace him further. I always talked to him in private. Once I explain the relationship I had in Christ, you'll understand my heart. The following pages tell of the food placed into my basket.

◆   ◆   ◆

Let's go back to when I attended my first church. I worked in the children's ministry and later became the director of the bus ministry. A team of bus captains would meet every Saturday at 8:30 a.m. A hot breakfast was prepared for us. Our minister of Christian ministries would train our workers on how to drive from home to home, bringing the children to Sunday school the following day. We would do follow-up with the parents the following Saturday and our teens would go and visit these families.

We would set up a time for our Evangelism teams to go as well. I felt a call on my spirit to join the team. As the years passed, I was trained to teach the class. God called me to the mission field to train others in how to share the Gospel. One year, I took my fifteen-year-old son to Mexico. I trained the local pastors there on how to win souls to Christ. Steven helped build a new church there. It was a real growing time for both of us.

DREAMS AND INTERPRETATIONS

I had a dream on a Friday evening that our church was going to divide. When I awoke, I asked God if this dream had come from him. If it was, I asked him to show me in his Word what I was to understand from it. I prayed and prayed for a long time. I asked God for wisdom and understanding. I started to read my Bible, and I turned to Revelations 3.

> To the angel of the church in Sardis write: These are the words of him who holds the seven spirits of God and the seven stars. I know your deeds; you have a reputation of being alive, but you are dead. Wake up! Strengthen what remains and is about to die, for I have not found your deeds complete in the sight of my God.
>
> Remember, therefore, what you have received and heard; obey it, and repent. But if you do not wake up, I will come like a thief, and you will not know at what time I will come to you.

Yet you have a few people in Sardis who have not soiled their clothes. They will walk with me, dressed in white, for they are worthy. He who overcomes his will, like them, be dressed in white. I will never blot out his name from the book of life, but will acknowledge his name before my Father and his angels. He who has an ear, let him hear what the Spirit says to the churches. (Revelation 3:1–6)

Saturday mornings were spent with the bus ministry. One particular Saturday, I went early to set up. Our senior pastor was there. I asked if I could talk with him, as I had something to share. He took me seriously because he had seen God working in my life before.

I told him about my dream and the scripture that followed. He received it as a confirmation, because God had given him the same scripture the night before. I had no knowledge of what the senior staff felt led to do the next day. The entire staff was planning to resign during the morning service. Pastor asked me not to say anything to anyone about what I knew. He also asked me to stay on at the church to help keep the ministry flowing. I had always been a volunteer, so I wasn't obligated to go. I would have been shaken to the core if God had not given me the news the night before.

The next morning seemed to run into the night, as I never slept. It was so hard to deal with what was unfolding. I went on ministering as usual the following day. This time, I didn't slip into the morning service. I knew I couldn't watch what was going to happen. What I didn't know was how the staff was going to handle their resignation. There were three church vans waiting outside with the motor running, ready to drive the staff and board members away. The pastor told the congregation the news and then asked them to bow their heads in prayer. Someone prayed with the congregation while the entire staff and board slipped out the side door, quietly and quickly. When the congregation lifted their heads, more than half of the altar was bare.

People were in shock, crying, talking—you can only imagine their response. I wasn't in the room, but I knew they were resigning. Yet the way they did it... well, it isn't for me to judge. I loved the church and the people in it. I ministered whenever possible. My growth as a Christian had come as a result of the faithfulness of so many who ministered to me in that church.

I felt like I had lost my family, as they all went stateside except for the board members. The staff members who left had been my mentors and I considered it a privilege to serve under their leadership.

three

DELIVERANCE MINISTRY

*b*ecause of my past, I was being pulled toward ministering in the deliverance ministry. Before serving in this ministry a person had better make sure it is really their calling, since it is one of the most difficult ministries. The deliverance ministry takes a person one-on-one with the demonic. Jesus is the only authority over the power of darkness and the blood of Christ is your shield.

My first open battlefield was with a young woman who had involved her life in the occult. Her home was full of books that taught her about witchcraft and demon worship, along with a great deal more. It is not necessary to write in length on this matter, as Satan doesn't need any glory or a foothold in our imaginations.

Our pastor called me to his office one day to tell me that this young woman had tried to kill herself. He felt led to ask me to talk with her. I believed that God would tell me himself if I was supposed to go, so I began to prepare myself through prayer and fasting. I felt like I was in spiritual boot camp. I can smile now, but I wasn't smiling then.

Then it happened. I got my marching orders to go to the frontline. Her parents asked me to talk to her and see if I could help. Could I help? I didn't think so, but I knew God was willing and able. I needed to be his vessel to do his work. That really took the pressure off me and the fear went away. God's Word says that we are not fighting against flesh and blood but against principalities. Suddenly, a spirit of peace came over me. I knew this battle would be fought in the heavenlies. I just had to show up and be the voice of our Saviour. The battle had been fought and won at Calvary.

This woman, who I will call Carol, had been transferred to the psychiatric ward of the hospital. She was a danger to herself. Earlier in the day, Carol had not yet woken up. The youth pastor had been there to pray over her after visiting with her parents, who were by her side. He then bent down to kiss her on the cheek as he left. The youth pastor had known her since she was a little girl.

When Carol woke up from the drugs, she looked at her parents and, in a man's voice, asked for this pastor by name. The parents told him soon after it happened. He was terrified. Before leaving for the hospital, I went into his office to minister to him. It can be very frightening to know that an evil spirit has called you by name. I encouraged him to read the same books I was reading and to search the Scriptures. He became wiser and his ministry became more directed as a result of God's leading. The youth pastor and I fell to our knees and praised God. We prayed together and I assured him, "You have nothing to fear but fear itself, so give it to God and trust in His protection."

When I arrived at the hospital, I asked to see Carol. The nurse said she had restricted visitors. The nurse stared long and hard at me. She asked who I was, and I told her that I was from Carol's church. The look on the nurse's face was indescribable. She said that Carol was visiting on the next floor, which was part of the same unit, but that I could go get her and bring her back down. She called ahead to tell them I was coming.

These two floors were on lockdown for the protection of the patients. The nurse asked me to come with her first, which I did. I was stunned by what happened next. The nurse led me to a conference room behind the nurse's station. There was a long table in the center of the room where they had their meetings. There was a small sitting area at the end of the room. The room had two doors with locks on them. The nurse told me to go get Carol and bring her to this room and lock both doors behind us. I was so surprised to hear this; Carol was a new patient, and they had no idea who I was or what Carol could have done. I was watching God at work. Even now, I still shake my head in awe.

I always had the fear that if I touch a demon-possessed person, that demon could enter me while in prayer. I know what the Word of God says about the armour of God, but knowing and receiving is not always the same thing. Now I needed to apply the Word of God and watch him at work.

I went upstairs, where Carol was waiting for me with her new roommate. I told her roommate that I wanted a little time to talk to Carol. We got on the elevator, as did a lot of other people. It felt as though a piece of paper would have had difficulty passing between us. Not once did Carol touch me, not even to brush up against me. It was as though God was saying, "Paulette, I'm right here surrounding you. You are protected." It wouldn't have mattered if she did come in contact with me, but it made me feel a whole lot better that she didn't.

I took Carol into the conference room and told her to sit down. I locked the door so we wouldn't be interrupted. The fear of Carol touching me was still in my thoughts, especially since we were going to enter into spiritual warfare. I sat kitty-corner to Carol. She had very long legs; when she attempted to cross them, she got halfway and then returned her legs to where her feet both touched the floor. You see, in order to cross over, she would have had to brush my leg. Again God was reminding me that he had everything under control.

Now why was I there? I talked and Carol listened. I told her about my experiences with the occult and the distraction my involvement had caused. We talked about strongholds, deliverance, and the armour of God—and how books, movies, and people are used against us. Then we talked about letting her lifestyle be given over to the foot of the cross. This was not going to be easy, as she had had several demons possessing her. She let them in and now had to be willing to send them out. If Carol did not want to change, it would be better to leave things the way they were, for as it says in Luke 11,

> When an evil spirit comes out of a man, it goes through arid places seeking rest and does not find it. Then it says, "I will return to the house I left." When it arrives, it finds the house swept clean and put in order. Then it goes and takes seven other spirits more wicked than itself, and they go in and live there. And the final condition of that man is worse than the first. (Luke 11:24-26)

I asked her if she would give her lifestyle over to the foot of the cross. To say a prayer would do nothing. Satan is like a hungry lion roaming the earth, seeking his prey to devour. We must give all things in our lives over to God, resist the devil, turn from our wicked ways, and then—and only then—the devil will loosen his hold on us and he will flee.

Carol had given her life to the "strong man" of Matthew 12. Now she had to demand her life back. Carol had a lot to change. The books she read needed to be burned, as there was a lot of power in their words. She also had to let go of the places she went to, and one of the hardest things to let go of was some of her friends. Carol and I went into battle that day, but it was no longer our fight; it was Jesus Christ's. Remember, never go on a witch-hunt, as God knows who is willing to give their lives over to him. He will send you if you pray, or he may choose to send someone else.

Carol was serving the Lord the last I heard and was attending Bible College in the United States.

TESTING THE SPIRITS

A young woman came to my church. I will call her Mary. Mary was an exceptionally beautiful young woman, though her beauty has absolutely nothing to do with this story. Anyway, she was full of wonderment and wanted to serve God. She found out that from time to time I was working in the deliverance ministry. She began to ask questions and convinced herself that God had called her to this ministry. Who was I to say she wasn't?

Mary's downfall was that she was detached from her knowledge of the occult. She had read about it in the Bible and thought that was all she needed to know. First you do this, then you do that—it was like a recipe she wanted to follow. She would call me up and say she was able to see demons everywhere possessing so many people. I began to intercede on her behalf. She was un-nerving me. I wasn't worried about myself, but I was worried about her. She was like a loose cannon, and she was on a witch hunt. I had our pastor talk to her, but it was to no avail. She had the answers and no one had a right to tell her what to do.

The pastor came to me and said that one of the board members who was singing in the choir had told him that when he looked down from the choir loft, he could see a dark shadow around Mary. The look of her face that day had frightened him.

Late at night, Mary called me with some news about how God had called her into the deliverance ministry. She said she had a vision where she saw a large field with a garbage dump in it. She heard God's voice telling her to go over to the dump to look for treasures. She said she had seen herself searching through the dump. Then she asked God what kind of treasure she was looking for. He said, "The dump represents the world and the treasures are lost souls."

Well, up to this point, if I didn't have any knowledge of what was happening, I could find myself getting pretty excited for her. I was praying so hard for discernment as she spoke.

I felt nervous while I listened to her. I was hanging onto every word, hoping I wouldn't miss something God would reveal to me. Then it came. She said she had seen the cross of Christ. It was in the middle of a field. She said she knelt down at Jesus' feet when a drop of blood fell on her hand. She said she began to weep, and Jesus said, "Mary, you never have to weep or ask me if it is I who is asking you to go into the world and deliver people from the devil. You never need to question again."

Wow! That statement took my breath away. I knew it would do no good to try and talk to her at this time. She was saying the opposite of what God's Word tells us. We must always, in all things, test the spirits. God will not throw us a stone if we ask for a loaf of bread, but we must ask. I began to plead for the blood of Christ to cover me and my family. I knew to stay away from her, and I did. She left the church and I never heard from her again. To this day, I don't know what happened to her. From time to time, I remember her in prayer.

WISDOM FROM THE SPIRIT

As it is written, "No eye has seen, no ear has heard, no mind has conceived what God has prepared for those who love him." God has revealed it to us by his Spirit. The Spirit searches all things, even the deep things of God. For who among men knows the thoughts of a man except the man's spirit within him? In the same way no one knows the thoughts of God except the Spirit of God. (1 Corinthians 2:9–11)

four
SPECIAL NEEDS,
SPECIAL PEOPLE

*l*ike so many other people, I have special needs. I
have a learning disability called dyslexia. As a result, I have to work harder and find different ways
to learn. When I went to college, I was turning forty
years of age. I had an instructor who identified my
problem and told me she was dyslexic as well. She introduced me to the self-help unit at college and they
began to show me new ways to retain the information I
was being taught in my classes. For the first time in my
life, I was obtaining good marks. I was so encouraged
by the results.

I started to work at a special needs school. I up-
graded by taking courses relating to the clients I was
teaching. After a few years, I was promoted to supervi-
sor, where I developed and monitored classes for our

clients. All the programs had to be approved by the government, which was involved with the upgrading of special needs adults. I'd had a desire to involve my life in this area for as long as I could remember. I believe this is because I understand the limitations and frustrations put on a person who has to live with special needs. I made sure all my clients knew I had a condition that made learning a little more difficult. I told them we *can* learn, but we have to do it differently than most people.

I know we are not to love the people we work with—favouritism and all that—but I did anyway, with no apologies. They taught me as much as I taught them.

There was a young student who rode the bus with me in the mornings. His name was Frank Carelli. He was so full of life; he made others around him laugh. He always had a funny story to tell, or he would talk about the latest movies he had seen. He knew about the actors' lives and what movies they had acted in.

Frank came to work one day and told us that his mom was very ill. We were later told that his mom had cancer. I met with Frank's dad twice during the illness and we talked a few times on the phone in relation to Frank's courses. This was a difficult time for all.

Six months later, Frank's mom passed away. Frank's dad came to pick him up, as he had on many other occasions. This time, Frank came into the bakery I was working in with some of our clients. He was very excited when he came into the room. He told me his dad wanted to say hello to me. I told Frank to bring him in.

When Domenic Carelli came in, I could see that he was a broken man. We greeted each other with a handshake and sat down. After talking for a short time, I asked him if I could pray with him and he agreed. My prayer was short, but I asked our heavenly Father to heal the broken hearts of his family. I also asked God if he would, when the time was right, bring the right person into this man's life to help him with his son. When we finished praying, I told him that this prayer wouldn't mean a great deal to him right now, but one day it would.

I didn't see Frank's dad again until one year later. It was Easter weekend and I was on my way to the airport. I was going to Kansas City, where I was to bring a very close friend's son back with me. This young man was in trouble and his parents felt I could help. I had been working on the streets in Calgary with youth, mostly with young people in the gay community. It would be a regular occurrence to see my living room filled with sleeping bags and pizza boxes lying about. I couldn't turn people away. I had the blessing of my pastors and worked closely with our youth minister.

So off I went to bring this young man home to his parents. But before I left for the airport, Domenic Carelli came by my work to pick up Frank. He had a bottle of homemade wine for each of the staff—and he had an Italian cake pre-packaged just for me. I was in a hurry, so I put the wine and cake into my suitcase and said my goodbyes. He asked for my number and wanted to call me when I got back. I gave it to him. My trip turned out to be a great success and the young man I mentioned returned home with his family. Shortly after returning home, I got a call from Domenic.

He took me out for supper. I remember I had one piece of dry toast and one egg. Domenic was so concerned that I wasn't eating very much (if you know much about the Italian lifestyle, you know that *Mangiare*—eating—is a way of life for them). I had just finished losing 110 pounds, so I looked pretty good and felt a little stronger. There was no way I wanted to gain my weight back again. You see, this was the second time I had lost that much weight.

The next day at work, Domenic came through the door carrying a very large box on his shoulder. He was so proud of its contents. He stated that he gotten up at three in the morning to make me several pizzas and fresh bread. The aroma was unbelievable.

"Paula, you will be sick if you don't start eating," he said. This is what every overweight person dreams of hearing—or at least I did!

He was adamant that I was not to share his work of love with any of the other staff. He said I was to freeze the baked goods and eat them for my lunches. He showed a lot of care and concern for my well-being.

After dating Domenic for a while, I found he had a tender love for the Lord. It was a simple faith, but I found it stronger than the faiths of a lot of people who had the advantage of studying the Scriptures.

Domenic reminded me of the centurion who considered himself unworthy in light of who Jesus was.

When Jesus had entered Capernaum, a centurion came to him, asking for help.

"Lord," he said, "my servant lies at home paralyzed and in a terrible suffering."

Jesus said to him, "I will go and heal him."

The centurion replied, "Lord, I do not deserve to have you come under my roof. But just say the word, and my servant will be healed. For I myself am a man under authority, with soldiers under me. I tell this one, 'Go,' and he goes; and that one, 'Come,' and he comes. I say to my servant, 'Do this,' and he does it."

When Jesus heard this, he was astonished and said to those following him, "I tell you the truth, I have not found anyone in Israel with such great faith. I say to you that many will come from the east and the west, and will take their places at the feast with Abraham, Isaac and Jacob in the kingdom of heaven. But the subjects of the kingdom will be thrown outside, into the darkness, where there will be weeping and gnashing of teeth."

Then Jesus said to the centurion, "Go! It will be done just as you believed it would."

And his servant was healed at that very hour. (Matthew 8:5–13)

It is such simple faith. All he had to do was believe in who Jesus was and the healing was done. Domenic had that kind of faith. He never read the Bible, but he had gone to church as a child in Italy with his family. He raised his children in the Catholic faith, just like I had been. He always told me, "Just believe and Jesus will take care of us." It was important to me to make sure Domenic had a saving relationship with Christ.

> For God so loved the world that he gave his one and only Son, that whoever believes in him shall not perish but have eternal life. For God did not send his Son into the world to condemn the world, but to save this world through him. (John 3:16–17)

> For it is by grace you have been saved, through faith—and this not from yourselves, it is the gift of God—not by works, so that no one can boast. (Ephesians 2:8)

I told Domenic that Jesus had gone to the cross for all mankind and that it is the only way to Heaven. God will never let sin into Heaven, and the Bible says all men have sinned, so how do we get there? Well, God looks at us through his son Jesus by way of the cross. Jesus took our sins upon himself and died in our place so that we could be seen by God as clean vessels. Jesus shed our sins into the bowels of hell, where they came from. When Jesus rose from the dead on Easter Sunday, the battle over Satan was won. All we have to do is give our lives to Jesus and accept the way of the cross. People say no one knows for sure if they will go to heaven, but we *can* know for sure by simply saying, "Jesus, I'm a sinner. Forgive my sins and come into my heart and life. Be my Lord and Saviour."

five

TESTING OUR FAITH

*d*omenic had prayed this prayer and I felt secure that he understood the way of salvation. A greater part of me believes he was already right with God.

Our family had a difficult road ahead of us. In October of 1998, Domenic was diagnosed with prostate cancer. Before Domenic's diagnosis, a friend of ours had come to see us one day and announced this same news. He was the same age as Domenic, so I asked Domenic if he had ever been tested for prostate cancer, and he said no. We both went to the doctor that week for a PSA (Prostate-Specific Antigen) test. We had a lot of confidence in our doctor and the test was processed quickly.

We were called back to his office at the end of the week. Our doctor gave us the PSA count and told us to wait a few minutes while he went next door and made an appointment with the urologist who took care of these problems. We got an appointment within one hour of seeing our doctor. God was truly in control. Domenic's PSA levels were not high, but his condition was going to be checked out just the same. The urologist gave him a check-up and presented us with two options. One was to wait six months and be retested, and the other was to have a biopsy performed. Domenic quickly said he would wait and come back in six months, but I said no; we needed to be proactive. We set a biopsy appointment for the following week.

Time seemed to be no obstacle. I was allowed to sit in a room with Domenic while the procedure was performed. The doctor took six smears from his prostate in six different spots. On one smear, he didn't have the instrument tight enough against the wall of the bowel, so a piece of tissue was extracted outside the prostate. This became the deciding factor in Domenic's treatment. Four out of the six slices were malignant and the slice that had tissue from outside the prostate was malignant as well.

We received a call from the urologist to come in right away for a consultation. Sitting across from the doctor and listening to him give us this news made us feel like we were in another time zone. I felt like I was robotic. I showed no emotion, and neither did Domenic. I wanted fact; there was no room for emotion. He was in trouble and we both wanted answers. The doctor had already set up an appointment with the Tom Baker Hospital to see the oncologist within two weeks. We asked our questions and left.

We drove straight to the Tom Baker Hospital, where I asked the secretary if there was someone we could talk to. She said we would be given a nurse who worked closely with our oncologist, who would have information for us. We had to wait a few hours to see her that same day, but the wait was worth it.

I would do anything for Domenic. When he went to this nurse, she told us we would need to do something once we went in to see the doctor. First, we would need to see the staff psychologist for a session dealing with this illness. Second, we had to read through a large amount of paperwork explaining the various treatments and their side effects.

I thanked the nurse and asked if I could have the written material right away. She was very willing to give it to us. Then we went to another section of the hospital to make an appointment with a psychologist.

The psychologist had a cancellation the following week, so we took the spot. Neither Domenic nor I showed fear. It was as though this was happening to someone else.

We had an hour-long session with this psychologist. He offered us many options, such as health groups, but we felt we didn't need them. After the session, I went to the hospital bookstore and bought a book that taught about all kinds of cancers and different treatments. I wanted to become familiar with the terminology so that I understood what was being said to us.

When the time came, we saw the oncologist. We were taken into a small room and our doctor's nurse came in to talk to us. She began to explain various procedures and pulled out a binder with the same information I had already acquired a few weeks before. I smiled and said, "Thank you, but I already have this information and have studied it thoroughly."

We had a little chuckle over my enthusiasm. "Well, I guess you are both ready to see the doctor," she said.

When the doctor came in, Domenic told him that I was going to be his spokesperson. Domenic was a man of few words. His grasp of the English language was limited, but he was able to express his feelings best through action.

Domenic knew I had his best interests at heart. I wanted to hear everything the doctor had to say. After he explained everything, we began to discuss treatment. Surgery wasn't an option because of the tissue that was outside the prostate. He had a large, malignant tumour on the outside wall of the prostate as well. We bounced a few options back and forth and Domenic decided to begin hormonal treatment that same afternoon. God is so good. He had to wait several weeks before he could begin his 38-session radiation treatment, but we both had peace over the wait time because the hormonal treatments would help to shrink the original tumours and kill off cancer cells elsewhere in the body. Domenic was to begin his radiation treatments in November.

To complicate all this, we were to be married on November 14. He was so sad to think he was going to put me through all that was going to happen. Over and over again, I told him not to worry.

We applied for early retirement for Domenic. The staff at the school board where he worked (as a painter sub-foreman) wanted to honour him. They threw him a going-away party. Domenic was respected by his peers and he wanted to say thanks for all the years they had worked together. His boss asked me if I would write something to honour Domenic at the party. His boss read it. I didn't attend the party myself, because this was his time. He was so touched by all that was said and done.

Here's what I wrote:

DEDICATED TO DOMENICO

On December 21, 1933, Domenico Carelli, the fifth child of eight, was born to parents Antonio and Domenica Carelli in San Andrea, Italy.

Education was considered a luxury for Domenico, and the opportunity to attend school was denied to him due to the Second World War. He completed Grade Three by attending classes in the morning only to return home and work for his dearly loved father on the family farm.

When Domenico speaks of his childhood years and their many trials and tribulations, he recognizes them as being the foundation for his strong character today.

Domenico and his family were forced into hiding when he was twelve years old, when the war broke out in Italy, placing hardship on his homeland. They had no warning that the borders in their area were going to be closed off for seven long months. The German Army occupied his region, putting his family and neighbours in danger.

Six families, including his, dug handmade shelters in the ground. These caves became home to thirty-two people. They listened to gunfire and daily bombing all around them. Food was scarce and their safety was threatened at all times.

Domenico speaks with pride as he talks about his mother, who risked her life to sneak out at night or during heavy fog, returning home undetected to bake bread for her family. "Never will I forget," Domenico says. "Never will I forget all the suffering."

Their homes were at the bottom of a hill which was unsafe for them to live in. German soldiers occupied the top of the hill and watched for the American forces to cross the Garigliano River. Six families lived in these holes and all looked out for each other.

These trials were the building blocks used to form the man Domenico Carelli, a man who today will never rest if he knows of anyone in need. He is a man of loyalty and trust, a man who is loved and respected by his family, friends, work colleagues, and neighbours.

When the war ended in their region, Domenico returned to work on the family farm for another two years to follow in his father's footsteps.

At the age of fourteen, he went to live on his own and to work 160 kilometers from home in Rome. He returned to his family monthly to give them a large portion of his earnings. He worked in Rome for six years.

Afterward, Domenico served a mandatory sixteen-month term in the Italian Army. When that was complete, he returned to Rome for two years before going to live and work in Switzerland for five more. He was wed to his childhood sweetheart. In 1962, Maria and Domenico made a nine-day voyage to their new homeland of Canada. With no grasp of the English language, two trunks in hand, and their hearts and heads full of dreams, they made their way to Halifax. A five-day train ride took them to their new destination—Meadow Lake, Saskatchewan.

Domenico's first job was as a cement finisher. After holding that job for three years, he took an apprentice course to become a painter. In 1969, he began working for the Calgary Board of Education as a painter. The job became full-time in 1977, though he had been a sub-foreman since 1972. The Board of Education staff became faithful friends, and remain so to this day. Domenico and Maria have two sons and two daughters who reside in Calgary with their families. Domenico dedicates his life to his children and other loved ones. He was also dedicated to his wife until she passed away in 1994.

Some people have hobbies, such as gardening—Domenico's gardening is his lifestyle. He grows his own grapes, fruits, and vegetables. His home-grown herbs provide a perfume for the sauces prepared in the Carelli kitchen. His plants are hanging in homes throughout Calgary and its outlying regions.

All those who walk through his doors enjoy his home. His greatest joy is getting up at 5:00 a.m. to bake bread and pizzas to place on the table as people drop by to say hello. His homemade wine wets the palette of many passersby. This is Domenico. He says he is not well-educated, but having the privilege of spending time with Domenico is an education in itself. We can take time to honour Domenico, but it is our honour to know such a man.

To my Domenico,
De soro mio Paula.
As I see you through my eyes
Happy Retirement December 30, 1996
Remember, you have two women by your side.
We will always carry you.
You will never be alone.

six

GOD'S GRACE

*n*ovember 1 that same year, I was diagnosed with a malignant tumour in my left breast. It was two weeks before we were married. I was scheduled for a complete mastectomy in early January, during a time when Domenic would be in the second half of his radiation treatments. I was more frightened for him than he was for me. He would come to my room in the hospital to bring me with him while he had his treatments. He would push me into the back room and the nurses would let me watch him on a screen, and I could talk to him if I wanted.

Our faith was being put to the ultimate test. We both went through the paces and trusted our family doctors, as well as the other medical professionals we had over the years. The same year as my surgery, my dad died of heart-related complications. My eldest son disappeared right after the funeral. Six months later, I had a heart attack and a stint was put in my heart. Eight months after that, Domenic had a pulmonary embolism, and then a stroke the following year.

It sounds like a nightmare; some people would say so. God never said life would be easy, but he promised to walk with us through our lives.

Domenic is seventy-four years old now and he is the love of my life. We are inseparable. He has a greenhouse in our backyard. He makes our yard look like a piece of heaven each year. There are flowers everywhere, fresh vegetables shared by all. He has a green thumb and enjoys teaching neighbours who inquire about how to grow things. Never a day goes by that he doesn't forget to tell me how much he loves me and the rest of our family. My kids are his and his kids are mine.

I am on permanent disability now. I've had twenty-eight surgeries over my lifetime. Arthritis is a daily battle for me. Some days are worse than others.

I searched my heart about what I could do with my time, so that I might still feel of use in the Kingdom of God. I feel committed to praying for others, and I have committed my time to writing this book. Domenic and I spent a lot of time talking about the past and Domenic gave me permission to tell you a little about his life and how his past is tied in with mine. Once again, we can reach into our basket of miracles and tell of how God has been at work in our lives.

◆   ◆   ◆

Going back to the war, when the German soldiers were occupying the top of the hill, they began to befriend the Italian families. Unlike the movies we watch, these soldiers did not want to be there any more than the Italian people wanted them to be there. The soldiers from time to time brought Army rations to the women, who would cook for them and share their food.

When Domenic was working for the Calgary School Board as a painter, he met a lot of people in different trades. There was a man there who he met off and on through the years, Louie, a man with whom he became friends. When we were married, this man and his wife came over and we began a very dear and valuable friendship. Louie helped Domenic build our greenhouse and we were able to spend a great deal of time getting to know each other. Louie would tell us of his past and how he had served in the German Army as a youth. You guessed it. Louie was one of the German soldiers who occupied the hill above Domenic's home.

Louie also told us how his platoon befriended the Italian families who were living in holes in the ground. These women would cook Italian food for him and his comrades. It was Domenic's mom who would wash their clothes and share their bread. It wasn't until many years later that Domenic and Louie met and became brothers in the Lord. They were an ocean apart, on opposite sides of the war, and both ended up making new lives for themselves on a new continent. How can people say there is no God? Things like this just don't happen on their own. His wife and I have become as close as sisters. They love the Lord and serve him. They have a son in the ministry. I praise God for their love towards us.

TIME OUT

Domenic and I have never been apart since we were married. Yes, we both spent a great deal of time in the hospital, but we were by each other's side through it all.

It's very difficult for me to be away from family. One of our sons, Steven, moved to Nanaimo, British Columbia. At one point, I hadn't seen Steven, his wife, or my granddaughter for a year and a half.

Here's an entry from my journal:

> March 13, 2008
>
> I'm sitting at the Calgary airport waiting to board my plane to B.C. Actually, I'm sitting in Tim Horton's eating a bran muffin and enjoying a great cup of coffee.
>
> Domenic wasn't feeling well these past three days, and I was concerned about leaving him. I felt divided about going.
>
> Last night, I had a dream that I was to take care of two men. One of these men was ill. I could see a man in one bed and then an older man in another. Someone told me that I needed to keep

these two men close to me. This person advised me to move my two sons' beds downstairs and make room for these two men to sleep upstairs.

Just then, I could see my two boys, and they were about eight and ten respectively. I knew they needed me. I said no to this woman, telling her that I wasn't going to push my boys aside and that I would find a way to take care of everyone. When I woke up, I felt at peace about going on this trip.

The first part of my trip was very relaxing. I was so excited to see our family. The commuter plane was delayed by one and a half hours. I sat next to a lady who was coming back from a visit with her children. We had a conversation that inspired and encouraged me. She was a mom of ten children. We talked about parenting and serving the Lord. She came from a small logging town and had raised her whole family to love and serve the Lord. She promised me that she would pray for God to intervene in my visit.

My trip was all I hoped it would be. Steven and I had some wonderful and constructive talks together. It was reassuring to think that this young man before me was wise beyond his years and that I could talk to him as a friend; I didn't need all the answers. My granddaughter Whitley was growing up to be such a beautiful young lady.

Saying goodbye was difficult, but I felt at peace. To God be the glory.

On the trip home, I sat next to a gentleman who ran a business. We talked for a short time, and then he told me that his wife was becoming a writer. I was able to inquire about a few concerns I had in regards to my own writing. The last thing he said to me was, "Paulette, *get published*."

BOOK
2

foreword

December 2009

After much prayer, I was convinced that my book, *A Basket Full of Miracles*, was complete, and I had already begun to write an autobiography of my husband's life. I felt the two stories were to be written independently of each other. Due to radical changes in our lives, I now know that the stories are closely interwoven.

The second part of my book is called *Break Away*. I was given the name in a dream. I say that everything close to us slowly breaks away. In the dream, there was a large mountain and large boulders broke away and began to roll down it. God told me to take my family to the side of the mountain so that the boulders would not kill us. There were others on the mountain who did not hear the voice of God and tried to climb to the top. The rocks crushed them. This part of the book tells me to keep my family to the side so that life does not destroy them. I know I will hear God's voice if I listen in a quiet place.

Break Away begins in the year 2007, when Domenic was showing signs of a debilitating disease.

Domenic drove me to an appointment I had with our family doctor. The office was located in the core of the city, making parking difficult. I was dropped off at the front door of the building. He was going to join me as soon as he parked the car.

I was called into the office before he arrived, but I knew Domenic would be waiting for me when I came out of the office. However, when I returned after the appointment, he was nowhere in sight.

I went down to the lobby and waited close to an hour. Concerned, I returned to the office to see if he had called. He was not answering the phone at home and I had no other way to reach him. After three hours, I called the police. They agreed to drive up and down streets near the building to see if they could spot our car. They checked with the hospitals, but no accidents had been reported.

Domenic had gotten himself lost. He drove close to the airport, which was on the other end of Calgary. He regained his sense of direction after four hours had passed and returned home. I was in tears by this time.

Domenic's explanation at first was, "I couldn't find a parking stall." Over time, the story unfolded. He couldn't remember where to go, because all the buildings looked alike to him.

These were the beginning signs that Domenic was having trouble remembering things. I reported the incident to our family doctor and he recorded it. There was nothing that could be done for him at that stage, for it was an isolated incident.

introduction

It has been asked of me, "How do people say goodbye to themselves?" This is a powerful but somewhat bewildering statement.

What becomes of the human will if you face life knowing that all the things you have done, felt, learned, or experienced will gradually be forgotten? Without mercy, you are forced to step back from what you have known and fight the daily feelings of despair.

You might often wonder if you have any importance to your family and friends.

At least, that's how Domenic feels now as he looks out into his diminishing borders of comprehension and understanding.

September 2009

Domenic, my beloved pillar, has been diagnosed with second stage dementia and Alzheimer's disease.

Dementia is a broad term that refers to the brain's loss of ability to function in multiple ways. It usually includes short-term memory loss. Dementia can range from being mild to totally debilitating, and in most cases the symptoms are progressive over time.

Dementia affects a person's ability to use language, speak, listen, write, read, and complete tasks. It also affects their behaviour and emotions. In the final stages of this progressive mental illness, people are bedridden; they no longer recognize or remember loved ones and they cannot perform the most basic functions to care for themselves.

There are over a hundred reported causes of dementia, of which Alzheimer's disease is the most common. Alzheimer's disease is caused by the destruction of brain cells (neurons).

My husband once said to me, "What value am I to you or myself if I can't do the things that make me who I am or if I can't remember what brought us together? How do I say goodbye to my beautiful?" (That is what he calls me.)

These emotions and fears are deeply seeded. Domenic has always been a man of great strength, with a need for order in his life.

I try to reassure him that he will always be the man I fell in love with and I tell him that God still has a plan for our lives.

I am reminded of Psalm 139:

> Oh Lord, you have searched me and
> you know me. You know when I sit and
> when I rise; you perceive my thoughts
> from afar. You discern my going out
> and my lying down; you are familiar

with all my ways. Before a word is on
my tongue you know it completely, O
Lord... Where can I go from your
Spirit? Where can I flee from your pres-
ence? If I go up to the heavens, you are
there; if I make my bed in the depths,
you are there. If I rise on the wings of
the dawn, if I settle on the far side of
the sea, even there your hand will
guide me, your right hand will hold me
fast. If I say, "Surely the darkness will
hide me and the light become night
around me," even the darkness will not
be dark to you; the night will shine like
the day, for darkness is as light to you.
(Psalms 139:1–4, 7–12)

I will try to remind Domenic daily that God is
bringing life and light into his world.

I need to address his opening words, "How do I say
goodbye to myself?" The answer is: "You don't."

With understanding hearts, we overlook his rapid
changes and remember daily, hourly, and often minute
by minute the man before us, who is and always will be
the head of the Carelli family.

I want to take you back to Domenic's life, which
began December 21, 1933 in a small village in Italy.

◆　　　◆　　　◆

San Andreas, Italy is a small town built upon the sum-
mit of a mountain. Winding roads make their gradual
ascent to the top.

These pages tell about how a boy and his family, all of them born and raised in this region. It tells how this family and others like it survived the war, and the trials they encountered when they left Italy and made their way to an unknown continent.

Over the years, I have heard questions asked and judgments placed upon older generations for their strong command of emotions and attitude. I, too, have questioned why they are so set in their ways. I have found my answers by listening to their stories. So many people I spoke to displayed complex personalities.

Just imagine having to start our lives over from scratch, learning how to forgive others who come into your life uninvited. The war years took their toll on all sides.

one

NAMESAKE

*O*ur story begins by introducing you to Domo.

Domo was the fifth of eight children born to Domenica and Antonio Carelli. They were a poor family who earned their livelihood by working in orchards that belonged to other farmers. They received a percentage of their income from the sale of the harvest each year. They were given as much food as they needed from the crops they grew.

Domo's parents would be called entrepreneurs in today's society. Antonio started a small business trimming grape trees. The grapes were harvested and sold by the vineyard owners to the local wineries to make quality wine for export, which was then sold all over the world.

Domenica, Domo's mother, was known for her cooking. The local villagers would hire her to cook for their families' weddings and she would cater other family functions that were celebrated each year.

The Carelli family lived in a cottage built in the valley at the base of the mountain. There were no roads that led from home to home. The land had to be cleared to make pathways. This was no hardship to them, as it was part of their daily lives. Roads were cleared around the boarders of the village to make way for horses, donkeys, and carts being pulled from home to home to deliver bread and vegetables from the local vendors in San Andreas.

Domenica and Antonio shared in the joy of their firstborn son. He was named after Antonio's father, whose name had been Domenico. It was important to pass on the family name onto the firstborn son.

Baby Domenico took ill and passed away in his fourth month of life. Losing him was devastating. They were not given a medical explanation as to why he was taken.

They decided to try again, and their second son was born fifteen months after the death of his older brother. Once again, they passed on the grandfather's name. Domenico was a strong and healthy boy, full of life.

He loved to help his mommy. They would prepare lunch together and take it to the field where Antonio was working. They would fill a basket with fresh homemade bread, hot from the oven. Large pieces of salami and fried peppers would make a tasty sandwich. Homemade wine would wash down Antonio's meal.

Domenico and his mommy ate goat cheese and drank fresh goat's milk with their meal. Everything, of course, was packed with extra portions of TLC—tender love and care.

After their meal, they would spend a little time talking about their day. This was their way of life, as it was for so many other farmers. The long day would fade as they gathered around a warm fire in the evening.

The Carellis had a fireplace in the center of their kitchen to cook on. It was also used to heat their home. There was no luxury of central heating.

Trees had to be chopped and logs prepared for firewood. The logs were piled high by the back door, making them easily accessible. The family would retire and sleep came easily as they rested their tired bodies. The next day would come upon them quickly, as it always did, and they would begin the routine all over again.

two

LAST KISS

*d*omenico was nearing his fourth birthday when tragedy shook the lives of the Carellis once again. Domenico was put to bed all cuddled up in his blanket and kissed goodnight by his mommy and daddy. This was a night like any other night. They said their prayers and went to sleep. The next morning, Antonio went to work in the fields as usual. When Domenico woke that morning, he climbed into his mommy's lap and said to her that she had to go bring his daddy home right away.

His mommy was surprised at what was being said. When she asked Domenico why he wanted his daddy home right away, he told her that a beautiful lady had told him he was going to die today.

His mommy reassured Domenico that this was only a dream, but he insisted that they go down to the field and bring his daddy home. His mommy saw that he was not going to settle, so she walked with Domenico to where his daddy was working.

Antonio was surprised to see his family there so early in the day. Domenico pulled away from his mother and ran to his daddy. Over and over again, he told his daddy to come home. "I'm going to die, Daddy. Today, Daddy," he said. "You have to take me to say goodbye to my Uncle Frank," whom he loved very much.

The family was feeling unsettled but did what their son was asking of them. When they arrived back home, Domenico was tired and wanted to take a nap. His parents kissed the little boy and Domenico laid down for his nap, from which he never woke up.

Once again, there was no medical explanation given to the Carellis for the death of their second son.

Two years passed after Domenico's death before his parents considered having another baby. Fear had a grip on these wonderful, giving people. The question "What if?" went through their minds. They certainly had reason to fear having another child.

Domenica became pregnant, and once again the joy of having children became a reality. They had a son and named him Angelo, and then a daughter, Maria. Domo was born four years later. His parents considered naming him after his grandfather, Domenico Carelli. It took courage to once again pass this name onto another son.

As Domo—or Domenico, as he was called—grew, his parents could see that he liked to do things with them. He had a similar disposition to his other brothers who had borne his name.

Domenico loved to work in the fields with his dad, and he was a natural when it came to cooking.

As the years passed, three more children joined the family—Alfedo, Atilia, and Joanna. The six children kept their parents extremely busy.

School was a privilege in those days. Maria was the only Carelli child who never went to school. She had to help at home. A lot of teens had to leave home and find work in order to help their parents put food on the table.

The Carelli children enjoyed playing with the children of families who lived nearby. They would join up with them and cross over the field to attend a little schoolhouse together. The classes were combined from Grades One to Six. The higher grades were taught in the city of Cassino, which was sixteen miles from San Andreas.

Eight Children,

Dom was 5th

Domenco I 4th mo. old deceased

Domenico II 4 yrs old. ✓

aria angello, son

Maria, daughter

Dome, 4 yrs later } lost six

alfedo

atilia

Joanna

three

IMPENDING WAR

*t*he people of the village, when going to the market-
place, were hearing rumours of the German Army
invading Italy. News was very hard to acquire.
There were no television sets at that time and radios
were difficult to obtain. Information and news usually
passed from one neighbour to another.

Antonio and Domenica decided to begin storing up
food and hiding personal property before the war
reached their region. Their home had little coverage
because it was in the valley. They needed to find an
area with more trees.

They found refuge in the base of a hill overshadow-
ing the valley. Antonio took his eldest sons and they
began to dig large trenches approximately three feet
deep and five feet long. They made a cover for the
opening by using branches and weeds that covered the

area. People passing by could not tell that the trenches were there.

While Antonio and his sons were preparing the trenches, Domenica and the other children prepared grains, beans, dried figs, and grapes to hide in the trenches. Gold and linen would be needed after the war to obtain money. They hid these things as well.

The war finally reached their region and the German Army began to take their position. A small group of German soldiers prepared a lookout on the ridge of a hill overlooking the valley.

The Germans were to report to their superiors if they saw any activity along the Garigliano River, which could be observed with binoculars; they were watching for American troops crossing the river, since the Americans had placed a military base of their own on the other side of the Garigliano, only a short distance away.

The villagers were given a three-day window to cross the river to the American side. However, these villagers did not receive word in time to flee. By the time the news reached the people, it was too late. The seven families who had no time to escape now found themselves on the front lines. The bombing began and they needed to take cover. They went and found a clearing on the hill where the German had set up their base. The men and children frantically began to dig seven holes that were positioned several yards apart. These holes were deep and the people had to slide into them. These dugout shelters were to become homes for thirty-two people during the German occupation, which lasted seven long months.

Two of these holes were dug over the nearby stream, which was to serve as their drinking water. The stream made the ground moist and cold. Their new homes were built in the slope of the hill, which protected them from the bombs that were dropped daily. The bombs would hit the ground at an angle, missing the holes.

At night, the villagers could see the blue sky overhead. The stars shone brightly, lighting their surroundings. The brightly lit sky and stars would soon be replaced by the smoke and dust that rose from the ground as American bombs pierced the ground. The bombs were exploding only a few feet away. The noise from the explosions became unbearable at times.

The German soldiers who were assigned to observe the Garigliano River took no pleasure in being there. They were just as frightened as the Italian families hiding below.

Some of these young soldiers came in contact with the families. For the soldiers, it was their first time being away from their own homes. They had not been given a choice as to whether they wanted to fight in the war. Like all military personnel, they were acting under orders.

The Germans and Italians were on opposite sides, but it wasn't apparent by the way they looked out for each other. Our good Lord was watching over them all. If the Germans knew when the Americans were going to bomb, they would, whenever possible, warn the families to protect themselves.

Domenico still has tears in his eyes when he tells me how his mother would go down the hill when there was cloud cover from the smoke and dust, or when the dew of the morning mist made it difficult to see. He was afraid he would not see her again when he saw the bombs falling close to where she ran.

She would return to her home in the valley to bake bread and make meals to take back to her family. She would combine the rations the soldiers gave her so that everyone would have enough to eat.

One morning, the bombing became so heavy that the soldiers wanted to take shelter in the holes below. They informed the families that they had to vacate their holes and fend for themselves. At that moment, the hard reality of being on opposite sides reared its head.

By the end of the day, the families were given the okay to return. After all, the soldiers were compromising their mission by being away from the lookout point. They couldn't see the Garigliano River from below.

four
CLOSE CALLS

*W*hile the German soldiers were occupying their land, it was Domenic's responsibility to hide the family cow. Early in the morning, he would make his way to where the cow was tied. He would feed and milk the cow. As he did this, Domenic feared for his own life, as he could hear the American bombers flying overhead.

Domenico could see the sun rising in the sky and wanted to return to his family. One morning as he approached the clearing, he heard a deafening explosion only a few yards away. The ground shook as a bomb dropped nearby.

Domenico remembered the training his father had given him, so he dropped to his stomach and waited in the still silence. He was terrified to move, but soon regained his composure and raised himself to his knees.

He crawled along the ground until he dropped into the hole, which for the first time he considered his home. When he passed that way the next morning, he could see a large crater in the ground.

Cathy Reale was a neighbour girl who lived just down the road from the Carelli family. The Reales' hole was situated next to the Carellis'. Cathy was the eldest girl of the Reale children. She was given a great deal of responsibility in the care of her younger siblings. She was a teenager when the war hit, and because of her age she had to be more vigilant than the other girls.

A new patrol of German soldiers passed by their area. They were much older and experienced soldiers than the one on the hill, and they were there for one thing only—to fight for their side. One day, Cathy was getting food for her mother to prepare when she heard the soldiers nearby. Cathy quickly climbed up a nearby tree to hide. She was carrying a large knife in her hand and placed it in her teeth while she hid herself in the branches of the tree. If Cathy was threatened, she would not hesitate to use the knife. Young girls were taught in those days that it would be better to lose their life than to let someone assault them.

After she saw the soldiers leave, she climbed down the tree and moved along the ground, slithering on her stomach to the Carelli shelter. The Reales' hole was several feet away and she needed help right away. Mrs. Carelli quickly threw a blanket over Cathy and placed tree branches on top. Mrs. Carelli then threw another blanket over the branches to make it look like a child's bed. The younger children climbed on top of the make-shift bed and played with their toys. It wasn't long before the new patrol came by and asked if there were young women in these shelters, but Mrs. Carelli didn't give her away. Beneath the blanket, Cathy had bruises on her body from branches digging into her flesh. She was cold and frightened, but also safe, and that was all that mattered.

Domenico lost two members of his family during the war. His uncle and grandfather were turkey farmers. A new platoon of soldiers once came into their yard wanting to take several of the turkeys to feed the troops. Domenico's grandfather lunged at them with a sickle and the uncle came to his aid, when a soldier fired his gun at both of them. He felt his shots were in self-defence, and both of the men were killed. After this, the family lost their confidence in the soldiers. It was a reality check for everyone. War was taking its toll on all sides.

After seven months, the military moved out of their region.

Starting Over Again

After the war ended, there was a great deal to do in order to make the countryside safe once again. Fields and roads had to be cleared of landmines, which were planted in caves, along the roadside, and in the hills. The mines made it unsafe for children to play outdoors or travel safely.

Domenico's eldest brother Angelo and his friend were walking along the road near a cave they had often played in before the war. The two boys heard Army tanks and soldiers coming towards them from the far end of the road, so they quickly hid in the cave. The soldiers were French, as far as the boys could tell. One of the soldiers saw the boys enter the cave and told them to come out. The boys didn't understand French, but they knew what was being asked of them.

Two of the soldiers went to check out the cave, crawling inside. Unlike the boys, who hid just inside the entrance, the men went further in. A loud explosion went off, killing both soldiers. One of the soldiers outside the cave grabbed the boys and threw them to the ground. He wanted them killed and shouted at the driver of the tank to run them over. A local lady came running to where they were standing and began to tell them that the boys had done nothing wrong. The boys lived in the valley. She told the soldiers that the German Army had occupied this region and had planted explosives in the cave. The boys were released.

There were so many changes after the war ended. Families had to be split up in order to find work. Property had to be reclaimed, and so many homes had to be rebuilt.

When the Carelli family returned to their home in the valley, they saw what they had feared. The bombs had destroyed part of their home. Part of the roof was missing—well, it wasn't missing; it was found in the middle of their kitchen, along with the wall, which had collapsed inward. Domenica had known about the destruction, of course, having returned to the home to make bread several times a week. She had chosen not to say anything, knowing that the family would fear for her life.

Families started to dig up the remaining food that had been stored before the war. Domenica started to dig up her personal belongings as well. When she opened the packaging that held her personal belongings, however, she found them gone. All the gold they had collected through the years from family and friends was missing. Her mother's linen was gone as well. She felt a profound sense of loss.

As time passed, the people settled into their old lifestyle. The ladies even began to return to the Garigliano River to wash their laundry by hand.

Antonio's sister-in-law had problems with stealing things. She was very good at stealing and seldom got caught. One day when Domenica was washing her clothes, she saw her sister-in-law a short distance away, washing her laundry. They greeted each other with a smile and a nod. Domenica noticed that her mother's sewing and lettering was in the corner of one of the sheets that the sister-in-law was washing. Domenica knew at that moment that she had stolen her personal effects. She returned home and talked the matter over with Antonio. They decided not to say anything about what they had seen at the river. They felt everyone had suffered enough during the war. Not a word was mentioned until several months later.

Antonio would chop wood and stack it against the back of the house by the back door. The pile of wood kept going down, however, even though they weren't using it. They couldn't figure out how this was happening until one evening they caught their sister-in-law at the back of their home. She had her donkey loaded up with wood and was ready to return to her home.

Antonio was normally a peaceful and gentle man until, but that evening he took a long stick and made a switch from it. He then started to beat his sister-in-law, showing no mercy. He ordered her to return every piece of wood she had placed on the donkey and stack it just as she found it. After she finished stacking the wood, he and she both went to talk to her husband.

Antonio knew his brother would not let his wife's behaviour continue. After all had been shared, including what Domenica had seen at the river, there was no longer any need for concern. Domenica found a basket outside her door the next day with her gold and missing linens. They never talked about it again.

Antonio found it difficult to earn enough money to feed his family and pay all the bills. It took time to get the farm running well enough to show a profit, so he decided to let his boys work the land and he went to Rome to find work. It wasn't long before he had to return home to his family.

Upon returning home, Antonio had a visit from the mayor of San Andreas. The mayor wanted Antonio to work for their town. The council voted to offer Antonio a large section of land to build a family home on. He would have to sign a contract to grow crops, fruit, and vegetables to be sold at the market in San Andreas.

This was an offer Antonio could not turn down. The profits would be his to keep. The land had to be cleared and the soil prepared and worked. His neighbours went to his side to help him build a home for his family. Antonio was so full of pride that the townspeople would trust him this way.

Antonio planted fig trees, grape trees, and vegetables of all kinds. For his family, he bought several chickens. They were even able to buy a few goats and sheep. The Carellis had a real farm of their own now, but money was still sparse as the children grew, and their needs were greater and Antonio needed help. Angelo and Alfedo had already moved away.

Domenico was fourteen now and he talked to his parents about moving to Rome where his brother Angelo was working. His parents didn't want him to leave at first, but they soon agreed it would be worth the sacrifice to let him take wing.

Domenico had very little education to fall back on. He didn't go back to school after the war; the schoolhouse was destroyed and the teacher moved away. Domenico had only completed Grade Three, but now he had to work at a job he knew well. He knew the land and he understood his responsibilities.

Angelo was working as a security guard on a large orchard outside Rome. He encouraged his brother to join him there. When Domenico arrived, the boys decided not to tell the owner that they were brothers.

Domenico met with the foreman and the owner of the orchard. He was firm when he asked for a job. The two men looked him up and down and smiled, saying they didn't think they would get a day's work from such a slight figure of a boy. Domenico said with confidence that he wanted a day to prove himself.

The owner liked his enthusiasm and agreed to hire him on a temporary basis, but they were going to pay him at a lower wage than the other workers. Domenico proved his abilities right off. He was experienced in handling tools and equipment. He was also experienced in working the fields, and he was able to manage his time well.

Before long, he was making the same wage as the other workers. The foreman took a liking for Domenico and taught him the business.

Domenico made the long journey home at least once a month to visit his family and give his parents a large portion of his earnings. He kept just enough to live on. His room was provided for and he could eat all the fruits and vegetables he wanted.

By now, the foreman knew that Angelo and Domenico were brothers. The owner asked the two brothers if they knew how to operate a dairy farm. The boys had very little experience, but they were both eager to learn. They were given the responsibility of preparing the cows to be milked. First they had to milk each cow by hand to draw the milk down, then they attached the machine and the milking was completed. The cows had to be cared for after milking and the milk had to be sent away to be processed. There was so much to learn.

The months passed and soon Domenico was given the opportunity to learn all areas of the dairy business, as well as how to manage an orchard. His abilities were noticed, and when the foreman needed to retire Domenico was offered his job.

Domenico was stunned. He couldn't imagine taking on such a big responsibility at sixteen years of age. He asked the owner if he felt the other workers would take him seriously. Domenico turned the job down at first, but then he was assured that he'd be supported all the way.

The owner and foreman called the entire staff to a meeting. There were seventy-five women and fifty men working in the fields. The owner told everyone that the foreman was retiring and that Domenico was their new boss. The workers were told that if they had a problem with the decision, they were free to discuss it now. Little was said in response. The owner said that if there were any grievances, they were to go directly to Domenico and he would speak to the owner. The owner was direct; he also told them that if there was any fighting amongst them, they could pack their bags and head for home. After that, things went very well.

Domenico was given a bike to ride around from one area to another. He didn't know how to drive a car, so the bike worked out well for him.

Domenico returned to the family in San Andreas whenever possible. He was getting older and had his eye on one of the Reale girls. Her name was Maria Reale, and she was very beautiful—even now, his eyes still light up when he talks about her. She had long black hair that flowed down her back. Maria was a quiet young woman. She stayed close to her family and learned all there was to learn about caring for a family. Domenico soon learned that Maria was everything he was looking for in his life.

Young ladies were not allowed to date a man without the consent of a parent or someone who could watch over their best interests.

Maria's and Domenico's love began to grow, but then Domenico was called to the Army. He was still working in Rome at the time of his enlistment. The owner told Domenico that his job would still be waiting when he was discharged. Enlisting wasn't a choice; Italian men were obligated to serve in the Army for a mandatory eighteen months of service to their country. Domenico welcomed this new experience.

Domenico reported for duty at Farderia Corizia, Italy. He settled into his basic training. The months massed quickly, but before long Domenic started to have physical problems. He chose not to discuss them with anyone because he didn't want to stand out in front of the other recruits. One day when the men were on a training exercise, he began having pain in his right side.

Domenico was being trained to fire a bazooka. It weighed a great deal, and along with his rifle and backpack the load caused Domenico to begin falling behind.

He could see the other soldiers in the distance. His sergeant noticed he was in trouble, so he ran back to where Domenico was and decided he needed medical help. He radioed for the medics to bring him a stretcher. Upon returning to the base, the doctor examined Domenico and told him he needed to undergo surgery to remove his appendix. Domenico had a high fever and the doctor feared his appendix would rupture. The operation took place that same day.

When Domenico returned to duty a few weeks later, he was assigned to work in the mess hall. Domenico thought of it as a cushy job with lots of perks. He knew his way around a kitchen and was a great cook. His commanding officers would come by and ask Domenico for extra portions of whatever was being served. He became popular with the other soldiers as well. He knew how to prepare home-cooked meals and the men loved to eat.

After his eighteen-month tour of duty was finished, he went back to San Andreas to see his family and, of course, his childhood sweetheart. Domenico contacted his boss in Rome and asked him if he would rehire him as promised; there was no hesitation. Domenico returned as head foreman. His boss kept the man who had worked in Domenico's places while he was gone. The farm was big enough for both men to manage together. Domenico worked in Rome for another five years. After this time, he gave notice and returned to Rome to marry Maria.

What a celebration the wedding was going to be! Domenico's mother was going to prepare the food. Maria's mother and the girls from both sides of the family helped Domenica with the planning of the meal and preparation of the wedding.

They planned a five-course meal that would begin with antipasti. The ladies made homemade meats and cheeses to be used in the antipasti. The second course was homemade noodles, which were served with fresh tomatoes and red peppers from their gardens. The third course was their main meal. They planned for two kinds of cooked meats, served with potatoes and vegetables. The meal finished with salad and fresh fruit.

Domenica made the wedding cake to serve the two hundred and fifty invited guests. At midnight, the eating began again when they served sausages, chicken, and pasta to all the guests and family.

An Italian wedding would never be complete without wine, of course. The two fathers made new wine months ahead of time in anticipation of their children's wedding.

The day of their wedding was filled with joy and togetherness. The bride spent her last morning at home with her parents, where her mom helped Maria prepare herself for her special day. Maria wore a long white dress that touched the ground. Her veil flowed over her long black hair, each meeting at the waist.

Domenico was at home with his family, preparing for the ceremony.

Maria and Domenico were married in the church they had attended as children in San Andreas. Domenico had never seen anything as beautiful as his bride coming down the aisle.

Everyone met at the home of the Carelli family afterward for the dance and reception. They danced and ate till dawn.

At the time they were married, it was custom for the groom to provide a home for his bride, and the bride was to fill that home with personal items and furnishings. Domenico and Maria decided not to follow this custom, because they had their sights set on moving to Canada when they had enough money saved up.

five

SWITZERLAND

*a*ngelo and Alfedo had already moved to Switzerland and established themselves in a career. The brothers discovered there were more jobs available there, so they asked Maria and Domenico to join them.

Maria was expecting her first baby. She was not feeling well enough to travel with Domenico, so they decided that she would remain behind with her in-laws until the baby was born. It was difficult for Domenico to leave his wife and unborn child behind, but they wanted a new home one day and needed to save the money they hoped to earn in Switzerland.

Domenico's first job was to work in a small bakery, delivering bread to the local people and businesses. He was given a room on the upper floor of the bakery, which he shared with the baker; the owner and his wife lived across the hall.

Domenico took a keen interest in how to make different breads. He paid close attention to what the baker was doing while he helped out by washing pots and pans. When asked why he came down so early in the morning, he told the baker that he couldn't sleep.

When the bread was ready, they hitched up the donkey to the card and then loaded it onto the wagon. Domenico would deliver the bread to the local vendors and restaurants in the area. The locals were so grateful to have this service at their door.

It wasn't long before Domenico was asked to become a baker's assistant, after which he was given a baker's certificate.

Sometime later, the baker took ill and was off work for several weeks. Since the bakery needed a fill-in baker, the owner asked Domenico to do the job on his own. It was a great opportunity for Domenico to prove himself. The owner helped with deliveries and they very smoothly.

Maria was due to have her first child by this time and she needed her husband beside her. She sent a telegram to Domenico to come home as soon as possible. It wasn't long before they had their first daughter, who they named after her grandmother, Domenica. To this day, there is pride in Domenico's face when he talks about his beautiful baby girl and how she looked just like her mom. She had dark curly hair and her face was like an angel's.

Domenico wanted his family by his side, but they both knew their baby needed a stable environment. Grandma and Grandpa wanted to keep the baby with them. Maria stayed with her in-laws for an additional three months to care for the needs of her baby while Domenico traveled back and forth between San Andreas and Switzerland. They decided that it was time for Maria to join him in Switzerland as soon as possible. During this time, they also made plans to come to Canada and join Cathy, who had already married and moved to Meadow Lake.

Domenico began to look for new employment, someplace where Maria could work as well. He applied for a job at the hotel where his brother Angelo worked. This job would pay better and Maria would be at his side. Domenico would work as the hotel porter. He enjoyed the guests who came into the hotel. It was the first time he met people from other cultures. It helped to affirm their decision to start a new life in Canada.

Maria was hired on as a chambermaid, and when the time permitted her duties included helping out in the kitchen. When the hotel threw a party, the staff was asked to help entertain the guests. They were told to dance with anyone who did not have a partner. Domenico and Maria soon earned a reputation amongst the guests who came to the hotel. The guests loved and respected them both.

Before one of the parties, the manager of the hotel called Domenico over to where he was and chastened Domenico for not dancing with more of the guests.

Domenico became angry and told the manager that he had only two feet and was only one person. From that moment, there was tension between the two men.

During one of the parties, one of the guests insisted that Maria have a drink he had prepared for her. Maria was not given to alcohol and not long after she began to feel its effects. She felt very ill through the night and neither she nor Domenico got enough sleep. Domenico told his wife to sleep a little longer and he would make coffee for the guests.

The manager took note that Maria was not at her station and went up to her room. He began to bang on the door. Maria did not respond, so the manager approached Domenico in the kitchen. The two men exchanged harsh words. Domenico told him that if his wife was pushed into something she did not want to do, they would both quit their jobs.

It wasn't long after this incident when the manager once again called Domenico to his office. He told them that a very important guest, a woman who had come to the hotel on other occasions, requested his company the following day. She wanted the two of them to go on a canoe ride around the lake. She asked if a basket lunch could be prepared for them to take.

Domenico was promised a handsome bonus for this favour. He went to the kitchen to call Maria over so that they could talk about this unusual request. Maria seemed all right with the idea, but she told her husband to watch himself.

Domenico met with the lady, who was quite a looker. She thanked him and said she was there on business. She was traveling alone and would welcome company for the day. Domenico picked up the basket lunch and a few blankets to lay against the bottom of the canoe.

The day passed quickly. There was much to talk about and the scenery was beautiful. In the heat of the day, the woman said she wanted to take a swim to cool off. She asked Domenico to join her, but he refused. It was apparent that the woman had her own agenda. Domenico told her that he was due back at the hotel, so they prepared to return.

Domenico requested to talk to his boss the moment he got back. He told him that no employer had the right to ask his staff, especially married ones, to perform such a task. He gave his notice, effective immediately for both he and Maria. The boss wanted to give him a raise and the bonus that he had promised. Domenic refused both.

six

Returning to
the Homeland

*P*reparations were made for Domenico and Maria to return back to Italy. They both knew it was time that they broke the news to their parents that they were going to move to Canada and join Cathy in Meadow Lake, Saskatchewan.

Upon returning home, Domenico found his cousin, Louie Bryce, visiting his parents. Louie had moved to Calgary, Alberta several years before. He was established in a home and had a good job.

Louie promised Antonio and Domenica that if their son and his family moved to Calgary, he would give them a place to stay until they could afford their own home. He had connections and felt confident that he could help Domenico fiond work. Cathy's husband,

Charley, had started working on the papers to sponsor them.

They updated their passports and everything was falling into place. They had spent months talking over their futures, and now it was finally within reach. The problems at the hotel in Switzerland had given them the push they needed.

Their main problem was leaving their families behind. The baby was very attached to her grandparents, who loved her like their own daughter. They had been away from her for far too long already and they knew the grief it was going to bring upon Domenico's parents when they left. Domenica was calling her grandparents "Mommy" and "Daddy" and shied away from her real mom and dad. She still slept in her grandparents' bedroom and the transition was difficult. Domenico and Maria decided to stay with his parents for three months to give everyone a chance to adjust.

Promises of their return to Italy were made. Domenico told his family that he would be away for five years and then would return. Maria carefully began to pack a large metal trunk that would hold their family treasures to take to Canada. She had spent a lifetime collecting, saving, and storing items which had become part of their identity.

Deciding what to take brought many tears. She safeguarded the linens her mother had embroidered— tablecloths made of fine linen. She had to leave so much behind, as there was no room to pack everything that was dear to them.

The baby's clothes took a great deal of space and only her favourite toys could be packed. They made sure they found room for Italian cookies and chocolate to give as gifts along the way.

Winter clothes could be purchased when they settled in their new home, although they had no idea how cold the winter months were going to be in Calgary.

The day was approaching and the family knew it was time to say their goodbyes. Brothers and sisters gathered together, wishing this day had not come. Domenic was the first child to leave home to go so far away. Maria's parents, on the other hand, had already said goodbye to Cathy when she had married Charley and moved to Meadow Lake.

There was gong to be an ocean dividing the families and the cost of travelling back and forth would be out of reach for most.

When the morning arrived, everyone gathered around the family car to say their goodbyes. They had to borrow one of the family's cars to fit their trunk into.

Domenic's parents drove them to the waterfront in Naples. There before them was a ship called *The Volcanic*. They had never seen anything so big in their entire life. It had three decks and there was a wide ramp leading to the first deck. People began to make their way onto the ship.

They both began to second-guess their decision as they watched Domenico's tearful parents while they said adieu.

Domenica didn't understand that this was goodbye to her grandparents, but she knew something was wrong when Nona and Nono weren't walking up the ramp with them.

They showed their tickets and passports to the staff, who welcomed the passengers on board. From there, they were escorted to the second deck.

People all around them were trying to get to the railings that enclosed the decks. All were waving to their loved ones or whoever had come to see them off.

Domenico found a clearing in the crowd and put Maria in front of him and he held his little daughter closer than he ever had before. He knew his little family was entirely his responsibility now. The people who had given him support were standing on the dock waving, with broken hearts, saying, *"Arrivederci!"*—"Until we see you again." The three of them continued to wave as the ship pulled away from the dock. Nona and Nono soon became small dots on the distant shores of Naples.

They began their ten-day voyage across the Atlantic Ocean.

It was time to dry their tears, pick up their bags, and go to their cabin. It had two bunks, a small cot, and its own bathroom. Maria began to unpack their suitcases, then they made themselves ready to go to the dining hall for dinner.

The other passengers went to their assigned tables. Laughter and chatter soon filled the air. People were making a fuss over Domenica; she was a beautiful child.

Her long black hair cascaded down her back to her waist. Her eyes were large and seemed to dance as she looked around at all the excitement.

The food was delicious. There was a surplus of Italian dishes along with food from their Mediterranean cousins.

So many of the other families were going through the same thing they were. So many people understood the heartache of leaving their homeland and families. As the evening fell, they began to share their excitement of the possibilities that lay ahead. New hope began to fill the air and they knew they had the strength of each other, along with their beautiful daughter at their side. They were young and strong. Neither Domenico nor Maria were afraid to work. In fact, they welcomed the new life that lay ahead.

They soon met other people aboard who became acquaintances throughout their journey. Their anticipation of a new life was accompanied by long nights of talking and getting little sleep.

Before long, the ten-day voyage was coming to an end. The ship was pulling into the dock in Halifax Harbour.

It was difficult for them when they landed, since no one could speak English. Charley had prepared a letter for them to use as they made their way to Meadow Lake. They showed the letter to anybody who was helping them reach their destination.

They were taken by taxi to the train station. Much to their surprise, the train did not extend all the way to

Meadow Lake, so they would have to travel the last part of their journey by Greyhound bus.

After getting off the train, they were taken to a bed and breakfast, run by a German couple who knew a little Italian. Of course, the Carellis also knew a fair bit of German from their years in Switzerland.

The owners were very gracious. Domenica was put to bed early and the four of them sat on the balcony and talked into the early morning. Maria told them how ill she had felt on the train from the food prepared for them. He, too, thought the food was dreadful. The bread used to make a sandwich had been soft and stuck to the roof of her mouth. She was used to the bakery bread that her own husband baked. She had never eaten canned foods before, having always made every-thing fresh. She couldn't imagine what other surprises this new country had to offer. The bed and breakfast owner graciously prepared a box lunch filled with fa-miliar foods for them to eat as they made their way to their next destination.

They were woken up at five o'clock in the morning, which left them with little sleep. Before they left, the German couple offered them jobs at their bed and breakfast if they wanted to stay. Of course, they de-clined this generous opportunity. Domenico and Maria thanked them for all their kindness and reassured them that they would be fine once they reached the home of Maria's sister and her husband.

They said their goodbyes and once again continued their journey. They boarded the Greyhound bus that would take them to Saskatchewan.

As the bus pulled into the station several hours later, Maria could see her sister standing on the platform. It felt reassuring to see a familiar face. Maria jumped out of her seat and ran to the open door of the bus. She threw her arms around her sister with a long, hard embrace. The time apart had seemed endless and their hearts had ached for one another's company.

The men threw the large trunk into the back of the truck and the women sat in the back so they could hold hands and exchange stories. They had so many questions to ask and stories to tell that everyone began to speak at the same time. Domenica sat quietly on her daddy's lap and fell into a deep sleep.

Cathy had prepared a feast to share with the tired family. The long journey had taken its toll on them, so they said goodnight after dinner and went to bed early.

In the morning, Cathy got up early to prepare espresso mixed with steaming hot milk and just the right amount of sugar. It was delicious and greatly appreciated by all.

The espresso was served with fresh biscuits and small cakes that had been baked the day before. They continued to share stories until Charley invited Domenico to go for a walk with him. Charley needed alone time with Domenico to tell him what to expect once he settled in Calgary.

"Life, as well as the way people act, is different there," Charley explained. "Life is faster paced, and people don't always look out for one another like they did in the old country. It is a good life with great people, but there is a difference."

Domenico thanked Charley for sponsoring him and his family. He told him he wouldn't let him down. Charley already knew Domenic and Maria were of good character.

NEW ROADS TO TRAVEL

Once a few days had passed, the Carellis knew their journey had to continue to Calgary, Alberta. Arrangements had been made for Domenic to leave Maria and the baby with Cathy and Charley. He was going to send for them as soon as he got settled. Domenico went on ahead to Calgary to join up with his cousin Louie and his wife.

The goodbyes were not as difficult this time. Everyone was full of anticipation of the coming months. Cathy and Charley accepted the invitation to live with Domenic and his family once they were able to buy their first home in Canada. Charley was a teacher and ready for retirement.

The family drove Domenic to the bus station and Charley made sure Domenic had a letter to help him communicate with others until he reached his cousins in Calgary.

As the taxi drove up to Louie's house in Calgary later that day, Domenico could tell that no one there had been expecting him so early in the morning. The driver and Domenico had difficulty unloading the trunk from the taxi. Both men put the trunk on the front lawn. It was too early to ring the bell, so Domenico sat on the trunk, feeling quite alone, and waited for the lights to go on in the house.

Domenic could feel the chill of the morning air as he sat waiting for the sun to come up. His mind was racing in all directions. He could visualize his parents' tear-filled faces as they said goodbye. He could also see Maria's face with the hopes and dreams expressed in her eyes before he boarded the bus for Calgary.

New challenges and hard work were no strangers to this couple. They believed in each other and knew Jesus was guiding their path.

A Reach of Faith

Domenic saw there a light go on near the back of the house. It wasn't long before the whole house was lit up and he began to see movement through the curtains.

A woman he had never met opened the door wearing only her night dress, having had no time to prepare herself for the day.

"Louie, Louie!" she shouted. "There is a man sitting in the front yard. I think he is your cousin from Italy."

Just then, Domenic shot up to his feet and ran to the front door and began to shake the lady's hand. At last he had seen his cousin and they greeted one another with the traditional kiss on the cheek.

Excitement mounted as they helped Domenic into the house along with his belongings. Louie and Johanna, his wife, had prepared the small suite in the basement for the Carellis during their stay.

It was Sunday and Louie had the day off work to spend with his cousin.

The two men made plans to look for work the following day. Louie took Domenic to a construction site where he knew a few of the workers and the crew boss. They gave Domenic a job as a cement finisher. He was also responsible to set the forms used to cast sidewalks. The weather was becoming too cold to work outdoors, so he was given work indoors cleaning and preparing the forms for when work resumed.

After a few weeks, Domenic sent for Maria and the baby to join him. They were so grateful to have this suite in his cousin's home.

Louie was foreman with the Calgary School Board and he supervised a crew of painters. Louie took on private painting jobs in his spare time. He would take Domenic with him evenings and weekends so that Domenic could learn the trade. Like all his skills, Domenic learned by watching, then doing. He has always had an eye for detail.

Domenic started a job at a construction site where he was given the job of tying lumber together. The lumber was then pulled up to the floors high above the skyline on a crane.

He was highly motivated just thinking of his family and their desire to buy a home of their own in the near future. He knew very little English, but the other workers knew what Domenic was saying to them. He would use hand gestures, like making fast circles to indicate that the load was ready. He would point up and down for directions. Many of the other men at the construction site, also immigrants, were in similar situations.

Shortly thereafter, Domenic had a run-in with the Calgary police. One day, he was put to work on the early morning shift and started work at 2:00 a.m. When he arrived at the work site, its gates were locked. A police cruiser had been following him closely on his way to work, and when they stopped to question him his heart was racing, as his English was not good enough for him to explain to the officers why he was there.

One of the officers called him over, but before they could say anything he pointed at the crane that was working through the night and said, "Me work, me work."

After the police understood what was happening, they waved Domenic on. He then continued on to the worksite.

seven

EXTRA INCOME

*M*aria wanted to help Domenic earn extra money, so she asked him if she could work outside the home. Domenic wanted to give her a chance to work in Canada, so he helped her find a job as a chambermaid in a local hotel.

Maria never spoke a word of English, but there were other women at the hotel who spoke Italian who were willing to take Maria under their wing.

Cathy cared for the children and did the cooking and cleaning while Maria was at work.

It wasn't long before Domenic told Maria that her job wasn't working out for the family. She was exhausted when she came home and had little time to spend with her children. Domenic said he would compensate by working weekends for extra money.

After the bills were paid and their savings were added to the money they had brought from Switzerland, they were able to send money back to their families in Italy.

Their First Home

There was a small house on a corner lot on Spiller Road. It needed a great deal of work, but the Carellis welcomed the challenge. Walls were knocked down, rooms were divided, and bathrooms were installed.

It wasn't long before this little house became the proud home of Domenic, Maria, and their family. They paid $7,000 and the renovations cost $10,000. This left them with a million dollar home—at least, so it seemed to them.

To hear Domenic tell the story, it sounded like they lived in a palace. They appreciated everything they had worked so hard for and gave God thanks for all of his blessings.

They sent for Cathy, Charley, and their beautiful daughter, just like they had promised. After that, Maria had her second daughter, Marisa. She was dark-haired with a dark complexion—*bella*, just like her sister Domenica.

Once again, the two families became one. There were three small children and four adults living in a 1,100-square-foot home. They were happy as a family and worked hard both in the home and at the workplace. They never forgot the sacrifice Louie and Joanna had made by opening their home and hearts in order to give them their first opportunities in Canada.

Now it was Cathy's turn to want to work outside the home. She had never in her life been in the work-force. She was a tenacious woman, having cared for her brothers and sisters in Italy. Cathy had always worked very hard to help her parents in the home, and she even worked in the fields, but she had little experience hold-ing a job. Cathy didn't have an education, but she is one of the smartest and sensitive women I know. Char-ley was very excited to see his wife take such a big step in her life. He was so proud of her.

Cathy was hired at a chicken factory within walk-ing distance of their home. She would leave the house early in the morning and return in the early evening to a delicious dinner that her sister Maria had prepared.

The tables were turned. The two families were liv-ing their lives to the fullest.

A SIGHT TO BE SEEN

The family would laugh as Cathy made her way to work. Cathy dressed like a person working in the Arc-tic. She put on heavy work socks, long underwear, and woollen undershirts—and then her clothing overtop! She tied up her hard-toe boots and wore a heavy coat and toque. Everyone around her would laugh as she waddled her way down the road. Cathy would exclaim, "I don't care. I'm warm!"

The factory, of course, was kept cool to keep the chickens from becoming contaminated during processing. Cathy's attire became an asset to her well-being.

New Horizons

Domenic was hired on as a painter at the Calgary School Board. He gradually became a sub-foreman and years later he was offered the job of foreman. Domenic was able to speak broken English, but was unable to read or write English at all. He declined the foreman's job but continued to work as a sub-foreman. Domenic was well-liked and respected by his crew. He stood up for his men and worked by their side. Once again, Domenic was showing his strong leadership qualities.

The Carellis gave birth to their third child, a son this time, in 1968. They named him Tony. There was so much excitement and pride. Tony would carry on the Carelli name.

Three children and four adults would present major problems to anyone's living arrangement, and so it was with Domenic and Maria. They knew they would have to relocate, as their home was bursting at the seams.

Domenic and his family would go for walks in their neighbourhood. At the top of the hill, four blocks from their present home, stood a large house built on three lots. It looked like a football field. In front of the house was a For Sale sign. Domenica kept saying to her parents how beautiful the house was, and kept asking them to buy it. They didn't need a great deal of persuasion;

Domenic and Maria knew this house would have ample space to raise their family.

An appointment was made with the owner, since it was being sold privately.

The upstairs had its own entrance. It had three bedrooms, one bathroom, a dining room, and a kitchen. The basement had a walk-out entrance. Cathy and her family would have their own suite on the lower level. Both families knew this house would meet all their needs.

The asking price was $32,000, but Domenic offered $27,000 and not a dollar more. He prided himself as a good businessman and was willing to see how the owner would respond. The owner told them that he needed the asking price because he had another house being built outside the city limits. Sharing this information was to the owner's detriment, because he made Domenic aware of his need to sell.

Domenic said that he was going to look elsewhere but still left his phone number with the owner. A day passed and then the owner called to set up another meeting. He said he would accept the offer of $27,000, but he would remove the fridge, stove, curtains, rods, washer, and dryer. Domenic told him he could remove the sinks and toilets as well—and he could also keep the house! Domenic said goodbye and left.

The same evening, the owner called Domenic and said, "Okay, you win. Come over and we'll do business." Charley went with Domenic to wrap up the deal.

The Carellis and the Bryce family moved into their new home two months later, fulfilling a dream of Domenic's.

He built a twenty-two by fourteen-foot greenhouse in the backyard. The house was built on a property that gave him enough room for a garden as well as his greenhouse. His yard became the talk of the neighbourhood. The two families were in their element. They created a little piece of Italy in Calgary. Maria and Cathy were able to freeze enough vegetables from Domenic's garden to last through the winter.

Time went by quickly and before long their family was to grow once again. Maria was expecting their fourth child, who was born on April 10, 1972. They named the baby Francesco. He was a strong and handsome baby, just like his big brother Tony.

The fifth and last child born to the Carellis was Frank. Maria was well into her forties and having five children completed their family. Unfortunately, by the age of four, Frank began showing some difficulties in his development.

There was no easy way to close this time in the Carellis' lives, because Maria passed away in November 1994. She was the love of Domenic's life, as well as all her family and friends. I will not write about this period, as it is a very private time in their lives.

eight
TWO YEARS IN

*t*he latter part of this book is written for the benefit of other caregivers and families who are looking after the well-being of people with Alzheimer's and other forms of dementia.

Two years into the illness, I needed to become proactive in Domenic's treatment. After the diagnosis, our family doctor contacted a neurologist at the stroke clinic who also specialized in Alzheimer's and dementia disorders. Domenic was given a CAT scan to help rule out other causes for the rapid changes occurring in his cognitive fuctioning.

I began to log significant changes and alterations in his behaviour and thinking patterns. Keeping an accurate log helped the doctors assess his diagnosis and track the progression of the disease, and he was being seen by specialists every six months for this purpose.

An Alzheimer's diagnosis is often made using criteria established by the National Institute of Neurological and Communicative Disorders and Stroke-Alzheimer's Disease. A diagnosis of dementia requires the loss of a prior level of functioning and ability in an otherwise alert and awake person. It will also include:

1. Measurable loss of memory.
2. One or more other areas of loss in the brain's ability to function (cognition).
   a. Language problems (aphasia), including:
      i. Finding words.
      ii. Understanding and following conversations, writing, and spelling.
   b. Problems carrying out physical tasks (apracia), including:
      i. Fastening buttons.
      ii. Putting garments on in the correct order.
      iii. Holding utensils.
      iv. Getting in and out of the car.
   c. An inability to recognize familiar objects and people (agnosia), including:
      i. Forgetting what different things are called.
      ii. Forgetting names.
      iii. Forgetting relationships and how he/she is connected to them.

    d. Problems that involve planning and organizing, including:
      i. Keeping a check book.
      ii. Planning a meal.
      iii. Driving a car.

INCIDENTS/ACTIONS/RESULTS

On the following pages, I would like to write about a few things that happened as a result of Domenic's deteriorating condition. For each incident, I will explain the action I took to manage the situation. I can't say my judgement and responses were always correct, of course; I can only tell you the results of what happened.

INCIDENT: I found Domenic in his bedclothes trying to unlock the front door in the middle of the night. He was unaware he was doing so.

ACTION: I installed a sound system on all three doors leading out of the bedroom.

RESULT: Temporary peace of mind for myself while I was sleeping.

INCIDENT: We were delivering flyers in our neighbourhood. He started walking in the wrong direction and lost sight of me.

ACTION: I conducted a neighbourhood search.

RESULT: I recognized he could not venture out of sight as he had lost all sense of direction.

INCIDENT: In April 2009, we moved into a condo in order to make life easier for everyone. There were two small trees planted in the front yard which Domenic did not like. He ripped the trees from the ground with his bare hands and started shouting at the top of his lungs. I hoped no one nearby understood Italian.

ACTION: I apologized to our neighbours who were watching this embarrassing display. I made them aware of his mental state.

RESULT: Empathy. Two of the three neighbours had family members with the same disease. This set the stage for compassion and understanding. Being open about his condition has proven to be helpful.

INCIDENT: We were in a restaurant for lunch. I excused myself to use the restroom. While I was away, someone asked if my chair was being used. Domenic responded by swinging his arms and flailing his fists at the person. He grabbed my chair and told him that it belonged to his wife. I was made aware of the incident when I returned.

ACTION: I apologized to the person involved and offered a short explanation.

RESULT: I have become very careful not to leave him alone in public places. I will try to go to a place that is familiar to him and where people know us.

INCIDENT: Domenic asked me if we were married. I was shocked and, I must admit, hurt, even though I knew it was not his fault.

ACTION: I found myself staring at him. I had no idea how to respond. At first, I shook my head, because I wanted to see what direction this conversation was headed. I immediately recognized my mistake and affirmed that we were married.

He replied, "If my children do not believe you, they can ask our lawyer."

"Domenic, they were at our wedding," I replied. Then I pointed to our wedding pictures.

RESULT: My negative response could have increased his level of confusion. I know now that I was on dangerous ground and I changed my response to the direction it was meant to go.

nine

FINAL FAREWELL

December 27, 2009

*d*omenic, Frank, and I were given an enormous gift from our son, Steven. He offered us the opportunity to take a final trip to Italy so that Domenic and his family could say goodbye for the last time. He wanted his stepfather to walk on the soil of his homeland one more time.

Our doctor warned me that Domenic's confusion would be elevated if I brought him into a new environment, but we went anyway. In order to help others, I must write what took place. When we were halfway through the seventeen-day trip, it occurred to me that I would never have considered going if I had known how difficult it was going to be on both Domenic and myself.

We started our trip at the Calgary International Airport. The day before we left, there was an attempted terrorist attack on an American airline. The news referred to the attempt as the Underwear Bomber. As a result, airport security was on high alert. Overseas routes were delayed two hours. We missed our connecting flight, and Domenic didn't understand why we weren't on our way. I tried to explain what was going on.

He repeatedly said to me, "Paula, I want to go home. We will try again tomorrow."

He had no concept of what prepaid tickets were and what was involved in cancelling a flight and the money that would be lost if we cancelled. Domenic talked aloud and wouldn't relax; people were watching him. When we boarded the plane, he was very vocal and had some inappropriate outbursts.

Once we were with the family there was no way to count how many times he asked to go home. I told him we were on a plane but he repeatedly told me to open the plane's door so he could leave. All day, every day, he wanted to leave. We made a calendar so that he could have a visual aid to help him know how many days were left before the holiday ended.

We were invited to one of his sisters' home for supper. He wanted to leave right away and return to the hotel that was owned by his youngest sister, where we were staying. Once again, he had a difficult time adapting to the changing environments.

People say they understand, but they really don't. We do take it personally, and that is normal. People understand the concept of Alzheimer's on an intellectual level but find its effect on their emotions hard to accept. I found myself defending his positions so that no one felt hurt—but this was extremely difficult because I don't speak Italian.

Early one morning, our family took us on a pilgrimage. It was held in a village that was a two-hour drive from where we were staying. Our son Frank wanted to stay behind with his aunt. Domenic became highly anxious because he thought we were driving back to Canada without Frank. It was difficult to convince him otherwise. That was a difficult day.

Terrorist in the Sky

The day came when we were returning to Canada. The family knew this would be our last trip to Italy, so the final goodbyes were painful for all.

We flew first to Frankfurt, Germany and boarded the plane to return home. The flight was supposed to take ten hours. Departure time was 2:00 p.m., and at approximately 2:20 p.m. the pilot announced that the plane would be late taking off. He explained that the plane had to be de-iced. After a while, I checked my watch and saw that an hour had passed. There was no visible activity outside on the tarmac. Once again, the pilot apologized for the delay and said that the de-icing machine had not yet been freed up. Domenic was becoming restless and demanded that we disembark the plane. I gave him a medication in hopes that it would help him relax and sleep for a short time.

Passengers began to stroll up and down the aisle to stretch their legs. Most of them passed the time by viewing a movie or reading a book.

I noticed two people who continually walked up and down the aisles. These people were observing seat numbers while looking long and hard into the worried faces of the passengers. They were trying very hard not to be noticed, of course, but I was convinced they were air marshals. I thought to myself, *Dear Lord, we are in trouble*.

I took Domenic to the back of the plane so that he could use the washroom. While waiting for him, one of the people who I had observed earlier was leaning up against a wall directly in front of me. Our eyes met with a quick but penetrating stare. He knew I understood what was going on, as I am sure others did as well. He quickly broke eye contact and once again started down the aisle.

Two hours had now passed, and passengers were talking amongst themselves, asking the flight attendants questions as to why they were delayed. The attendants were well-trained, providing information and helping to calm people's fears. They told us that this was common practice in the cold weather. Flights were always delayed due to icing. The problem was that it was not cold out; the temperature was $-3°C$ and there was no snow.

At approximately 3:40 p.m., two additional air marshals boarded the plane. At least, I assumed they were air marshals dressed in civilian clothing. The four grouped together for a moment, then divided into two groups. Each group removed two passengers, one on either side of the plane.

I looked into the face of one of the young men who was being escorted off the aircraft. He was in his early twenties, if not younger. He said to the air marshal, "Do I have to take all my belongings?"

"Yes," was his reply. They then left the plane. Minutes later, a third man was taken off. He was sitting directly in front of me.

I watched as a father and mother of three small children began to gather their belongings. The father placed one little boy under his arm and hung onto his carry-on baggage. With the other hand, he pushed his little girl towards the exit of the plane. The mother quickly picked up her other child and the five of them left the plane as quickly as they could. Two other people from our area also departed the plane.

The pilot came on the intercom and explained that we were encountering a situation beyond our control. All passengers had to return to their seats immediately. All washrooms were to be cleared as well.

Moments later, the police came aboard. I noticed two types of uniforms. The authorities began to check passengers according to their assigned seat. They opened handbags which had been taken aboard the plane. We were being looked at long and hard as each row was searched.

A trained dog made its way aboard. The dog was taken to the back of the plane. Frank and Domenic had no idea about what was transpiring. I was very concerned that Domenic would say something that would get us into trouble. He wanted to climb over the seats in order to leave the plane.

The police blocked the aisles and there was to way to the back of the plane. Frank wanted to pet the dog. What a nightmare!

I *prayed* and *prayed* for God to help us. To *help me* to know how to keep Domenic quiet. Just think, we hadn't even left the airport and there was still a long flight ahead of us.

We were now into our fourth hour and still on the tarmac in Frankfurt.

The young man who had been removed from the plane, the one seated in front of us, was allowed to return to the plane. I felt sorry for him; a couple across the aisle was pointing at him, saying that he was the one who had been removed. He must have felt so violated.

The pilot announced then that we were all to collect our belongings. We were going to be taken to an area just outside the plane which we were not to leave. The pilot said that the plane was going to be swept and that it would take another forty-five minutes. There was police standing at the exit areas where we were waiting.

Another two dogs were walking around us and going through the washrooms, sniffing our carry-on baggage.

The passengers were sullen, watching what was happening around us and what was going to happen next. It was well into the fourth hour when we were given the okay to once again board the plane.

Several seats were empty and people relocated themselves into the vacated seats as we prepared for the long journey home. Once again, the pilot made an announcement. This time, his voice did not sound strong and in control. He had a slight quiver in his voice, like anybody would expect. He thanked us for being patient—as if we had a choice! He said that the doors were secure and that we would taxi out shortly. We were told that there would be an additional short delay while the baggage handlers removed the suitcases belonging to the passengers who had decided not to fly with us on our journey to Canada.

I'm sure many—myself included—would have welcomed the chance not to take this flight. The choice was not mine, however, since time was an obstacle.

Domenic had regressed dramatically during our time in Italy and a five-hour delay added fuel to the problematic fire of getting my family back home.

Our plane finally began to taxi down the runway. I looked around and saw a young girl somewhere between sixteen and eighteen years old. She was holding her mom's hand from across the aisle and looked frightened. Many people were expecting the worst upon takeoff. After all, technology is advanced enough that someone can be sitting elsewhere and press a detonator button, if they know what they're doing. The bags in the cargo hold were not well-screened and could easily hold plastic devices. *But by God's grace so go I!* My faith was once again put to the ultimate test.

A vivid imagination can take its toll on one's well-being. Speaking for myself, I began to questions the motives of other passengers. We had been in the air for approximately four hours when a man across from me got up and proceeded to the back of the plane. I assumed he was using the restroom. Moments later, a young man was walking quickly towards the back of the plane carrying an open laptop. The plane hit some turbulence at that moment, causing the man to lose his balance. He then rested the laptop on the seat across from me to steady it. He regained his balance and the man from the back returned to his seat. This, in turn, caused the man with the laptop to turn around and hasten to the front of the plane.

He was clutching the laptop to his chest. This was the first time I felt panic on the inside. I began having angina pains in my chest (I knew they were angina pains because I'd had a heart attack in 2001).

At the same time this happened, I sat in my seat watching Domenic trying to feed his ice cream to the guinea pigs on the television screen in front of him. He thought they were real and began to pet the screen. I didn't know how to react to either my out-of-control imagination or the reality before me. I was concerned about the possible reasons a man might want to take an open laptop to the restroom and then rush back to his seat. My second concern was for Domenic, who was at that moment in a world of his own and could quickly become uncontrollable if I left my seat to talk to someone.

The ten-hour flight took its toll on the passengers and staff. When we finally landed at the Calgary International Airport, Domenic, Frank, and I waited until the other passengers had gotten off the plane. When it was our turn, we started down the aisle—just as the pilot was making his way to the back of the plane. He stopped for a moment to address those few of us who hadn't left yet, thanking us for our patience. We began thanking him for getting us home in one piece.

Do I regret being in Italy? No. Domenic's family needed to say their goodbyes, as a family, to their brother one last time. Only God knows the future.

i hope this helps

Since I finished my book, Domenic, Frank, and I have moved to Nanaimo, British Columbia. We live in a small condo that we bought from our son, Steven. We look over the inlet leading to the ocean. We spend hours watching the small boats make their way up and down the harbour. We can see the Departure Bay Fair set sail every few hours and return to dock. It's a dream come true for us.

My desk sits in front of the window and I can see the other side of the harbour light up. If I have my window open, I can hear the seagulls flying about. The feel of the ocean winds coming into my room makes me feel alive. I look over at my darling Domenic as he sleeps so peacefully and I praise my Father above for making a way for us to live out our lives in such a beautiful piece of heaven here on earth. Spectacular, peaceful, inviting. It is like being at a resort every day.

The best thing of all is that we found a church that's only a ten-minute walk from our door. When our pastor visits us, he walks down. How great is that? Our church family already understands our situation and has taken us under their wing. Domenic hums to the songs as we sing praises to God and I have seen him raise his hand toward the heavens. These are small blessings, but they strengthen me. The church family and our pastor watch over Frank and help fill his days whenever possible. Frank is happy here as well.

For me? Well, I have come home!